D0461181

WILLIAMS-SONOMA

FOODMADEFAST
baking

RECIPES

Lou Seibert Pappas

GENERAL EDITOR

Chuck Williams

PHOTOGRAPHY

Tucker + Hossler

Oxmoor House®

contents

30 MINUTES START TO FINISH

15 MINUTES HANDS-ON TIME

MAKE MORE TO STORE

about this book

The buttery aroma of cookies in the oven. The last lick of batter off the spoon. Baking at home is a little bit magical, transforming the simplest ingredients—a scoop of sugar, a cup of flour, some butter and eggs—into any number of delightful treats. But if you're like most people, you have little time to spend in the kitchen, even as you care more than ever about the quality and flavor of the food you eat.

The recipes in these pages are designed to show you how to bake smarter, so you spend less time in the kitchen. With helpful guidelines for planning your shopping, stocking your pantry, and getting your prep work done quickly and easily, *Baking* shows how to whip up a batch of muffins or a delicious homemade cake, often in less than 30 minutes. Taken together, these recipes add up to a smarter way to think about baking—and show how making good food from scratch can fit into our busy schedules.

Chuck

30 minutes
start to finish

butter
pecan cookies

Unsalted butter,
4 tablespoons (2 oz/60 g),
at room temperature

Powdered (icing) sugar,
⅓ cup (1½ oz/45 g), plus
extra for dusting

Vanilla extract (essence),
1 teaspoon

Salt, ¼ teaspoon

Flour, 1½ cups (7½ oz/
235 g)

Pecans, ¾ cup (3 oz/90 g)
toasted and finely chopped

MAKES ABOUT
36 COOKIES

1 Prepare the baking sheets
Position a rack in the middle of the oven and preheat
to 325°F (165°C). Line 2 rimless baking sheets with parchment
(baking) paper.

2 Mix the dough
In a large bowl, using an electric mixer on medium
speed, beat the butter and ⅓ cup powdered sugar until creamy.
Add the vanilla, salt, and flour and mix until blended. Add the
pecans and mix until evenly distributed.

3 Bake the cookies
With floured hands, shape the dough into ¾-inch (2-cm)
balls and place on the prepared sheets, spacing them about
1½ inches (4 cm) apart. Bake until the cookies are very light
brown, 15–18 minutes. Let the cookies cool on the baking
sheets on wire racks for 10 minutes. Slide the parchment with
the cookies onto a work surface and dust with powdered sugar
shaken through a sieve. Let cool completely.

cook's tip

Slivered almonds or hazelnuts
(filberts) may be used in place
of pecans in these nutty butter
cookies. To remove the skins
from whole hazelnuts, toast them
in a frying pan over medium
heat, stirring often, until they are
fragrant and golden brown, about
10 minutes. Rub the warm nuts
in a kitchen towel to loosen the
skins (don't worry if tiny bits of
skin are still attached), then chop.

cook's tip

Parchment (baking) paper has a nonstick surface that can withstand the intense heat of the oven. It is removed from the pans after use and discarded, facilitating cleanup. If you cannot find parchment paper, do not substitute waxed paper. Instead, grease the pans with butter.

ginger-molasses cookies

1 **Prepare the baking sheets**
Position a rack in the middle of the oven and preheat to 350°F (180°C). Line 2 rimless baking sheets with parchment (baking) paper.

2 **Mix the dough**
In a large bowl, using an electric mixer on medium speed, beat the butter and sugar until creamy. Add the egg and molasses and beat until smooth. In another bowl, stir together the flour, baking soda, salt, ginger, cinnamon, and allspice. Add the dry ingredients to the wet ingredients and mix on low speed until blended.

3 **Bake the cookies**
Drop level tablespoonfuls of the dough onto the prepared sheets, spacing them about 2 inches (5 cm) apart. Bake until the cookies are browned and firm to the touch, 10–12 minutes. Let the cookies cool on the baking sheets on wire racks for 5 minutes, then transfer to wire racks to cool completely.

Unsalted butter, 3/4 cup (6 oz/185 g), at room temperature

Light brown sugar, 1 cup (7 oz/220 g) firmly packed

Egg, 1

Light molasses, 1/3 cup (3 1/2 oz/105 g)

Flour, 2 cups (10 oz/315 g)

Baking soda (bicarbonate of soda), 1 1/2 teaspoons

Salt, 1/4 teaspoon

Ground ginger, 1 teaspoon

Ground cinnamon, 1 teaspoon

Ground allspice, 1/2 teaspoon

MAKES ABOUT
40 COOKIES

oatmeal–chocolate chip cookies

Unsalted butter, 1 cup
(8 oz/250 g)

Granulated sugar, ¾ cup
(6 oz/185 g)

Light brown sugar, ¾ cup
(6 oz/185 g) firmly packed

Eggs, 2

Vanilla extract (essence),
1 teaspoon

Flour, 1½ cups (7½ oz/
235 g)

**Baking soda (bicarbonate
of soda),** 1 teaspoon

Salt, ¼ teaspoon

Old-fashioned rolled oats,
2 cups (6 oz/185 g)

**Semisweet (plain) or
bittersweet chocolate
chips,** 12 oz (375 g)

Walnuts, 1 cup (4 oz/
125 g) toasted and chopped
(optional)

MAKES ABOUT
60 COOKIES

1 **Prepare the baking sheets**
Position a rack in the middle of the oven and preheat
to 350°F (180°C). Line 2 rimless baking sheets with parchment
(baking) paper.

2 **Mix the dough**
In a large bowl, using an electric mixer on medium
speed, beat the butter and granulated and brown sugars until
creamy. Add the eggs and vanilla and beat until smooth. In
another bowl, stir together the flour, baking soda, and salt. Add
the dry ingredients to the wet ingredients and beat on low
speed until smooth. Stir in the oatmeal, chocolate chips, and
walnuts, if using.

3 **Bake the cookies**
Drop rounded tablespoonfuls of the dough onto the
prepared sheets, spacing them about 1½ inches (4 cm) apart.
Bake until the cookies are golden brown, 10–12 minutes.
Transfer the cookies to wire racks to cool completely.

cook's tip

You can toast nuts in advance
so that you have them on hand.
Spread the walnuts in a single
layer on a baking sheet and toast
in a preheated 325°F (165°C)
oven, stirring occasionally, until
fragrant, about 10 minutes. Store
in an airtight container in the
refrigerator for up to 5 days or
in the freezer for up to 1 month.

chocolate
brownie cookies

1 **Prepare the baking sheets**
Position a rack in the middle of the oven and preheat to 350°F (180°C). Line 2 rimless baking sheets with parchment (baking) paper.

2 **Mix the dough**
In a heavy saucepan over low heat, melt together the butter and chocolate, stirring constantly. Remove from the heat. Stir in the brown sugar, eggs, and vanilla. Stir in the flour and baking powder until blended. Stir in the walnuts, if using, until evenly distributed. Refrigerate the dough for 4–5 minutes.

3 **Bake the cookies**
Drop rounded tablespoonfuls of the dough onto the prepared sheets, spacing them about 1½ inches (4 cm) apart. Bake until the cookies are set but still slightly soft in the center, 10–12 minutes. Transfer the cookies to wire racks to cool.

Unsalted butter,
4 tablespoons (2 oz/60 g)

Semisweet (plain) or bittersweet chocolate,
12 oz (375 g), chopped

Light brown sugar, ¾ cup
(6 oz/185 g) firmly packed

Eggs, 2

Vanilla extract (essence),
1 teaspoon

Flour, ½ cup (2½ oz/75 g)

Baking powder, ¼ teaspoon

Walnuts, 1½ cups (6½ oz/
200 g) toasted and chopped
(optional)

MAKES ABOUT
36 COOKIES

17

cheddar-chive biscuits

Flour, 2 cups (10 oz/315 g)

Baking powder, 2½ teaspoons

Salt, ½ teaspoon

Extra-sharp Cheddar cheese, ½ cup (2 oz/60 g) finely shredded

Fresh chives, ¼ cup (⅓ oz/ 10 g) minced

Unsalted butter, 6 tablespoons (3 oz/90 g) cold, cut into cubes

Milk, ¾ cup (6 fl oz/180 ml)

MAKES 12 BISCUITS

1 **Prepare the baking sheet**
Position a rack in the middle of the oven and preheat to 425°F (220°C). Line a rimless baking sheet with parchment (baking) paper.

2 **Mix the dough**
In a large bowl, stir together the flour, baking powder, salt, cheese, and chives. Using a pastry blender or 2 knives, cut in the butter until the mixture forms coarse crumbs about the size of peas. Add the milk to the dry ingredients and, using a rubber spatula, stir just until evenly moistened.

3 **Shape and bake the biscuits**
Turn out the dough onto a lightly floured work surface and press together gently. Knead the dough about 6 times and form into a ball. Pat into a circle about ¾ inch (2 cm) thick. Using a floured 3-inch (7.5-cm) round biscuit cutter, cut out rounds and place them on the prepared sheet, spacing them about 1 inch (2.5 cm) apart. Gather the scraps, pat out again, and cut out more biscuits. Bake until the biscuits are golden brown, 15–18 minutes. Transfer to a wire rack and let cool slightly, then serve.

cook's tip

To make classic buttermilk biscuits, omit the cheese and chives and substitute ¾ cup (6 fl oz/180 ml) buttermilk for the milk. Decrease the baking powder to 2 teaspoons and add ½ teaspoon baking soda (bicarbonate of soda). Proceed as directed.

cook's tip

You can top the muffin batter with a coarse sugar, such as Demerara or turbinado, before baking. Or, you can sprinkle the batter with leftover streusel topping or chopped toasted nuts mixed with brown sugar.

raspberry-lemon muffins

1 Prepare the muffin pan

Position a rack in the middle of the oven and preheat to 425°F (220°C). Line 12 standard muffin cups with paper liners.

2 Mix the batter

In a large bowl, stir together the flour, baking powder, baking soda, salt, and nutmeg. In another bowl, whisk together the eggs and sugar until blended. Whisk in the milk, butter, and lemon zest. Add the wet ingredients to the dry ingredients and, using a rubber spatula, stir just until evenly moistened. Gently fold in the raspberries just until evenly distributed.

3 Bake the muffins

Spoon the batter into the prepared muffin cups, filling them three-quarters full. Bake until the muffins are golden brown and a toothpick inserted into the center of a muffin comes out clean, 15–18 minutes. Let the muffins cool in the pan on a wire rack for 5 minutes. Transfer the muffins to the wire rack, let cool briefly, and serve.

Flour, 2 cups (10 oz/315 g)

Baking powder, 2 teaspoons

Baking soda (bicarbonate of soda), 1/2 teaspoon

Salt, 1/4 teaspoon

Ground nutmeg, 1/4 teaspoon

Eggs, 2

Light brown sugar, 2/3 cup (5 oz/155 g) firmly packed

Milk, 1 cup (8 fl oz/250 ml)

Unsalted butter, 6 tablespoons (3 oz/90 g), melted

Lemon zest, 1 tablespoon finely grated

Raspberries or blueberries, 1 cup (4 oz/125 g) fresh or frozen

MAKES 12 MUFFINS

21

spiced carrot muffins

Flour, 2 cups (10 oz/315 g)

Baking powder, 2 teaspoons

Baking soda (bicarbonate of soda), ½ teaspoon

Salt, ¼ teaspoon

Ground cinnamon, 1 teaspoon

Eggs, 2

Light brown sugar, ⅔ cup (5 oz/155 g) firmly packed

Buttermilk or sour cream, 1 cup (8 fl oz/250 ml)

Unsalted butter, 6 tablespoons (3 oz/90 g), melted

Carrots, 2 large, finely shredded (1½ cups/5 oz/155 g)

Raisins, dried currants, or golden raisins (sultanas), ½ cup (2 oz/60 g) (optional)

MAKES 12 MUFFINS

1 **Prepare the muffin pan**
Position a rack in the middle of the oven and preheat to 425°F (220°C). Line 12 standard muffin cups with paper liners.

2 **Mix the batter**
In a large bowl, stir together the flour, baking powder, baking soda, salt, and cinnamon. In another bowl, whisk together the eggs and brown sugar until blended. Whisk in the buttermilk and melted butter. Add the wet ingredients to the dry ingredients and, using a rubber spatula, stir just until evenly moistened. Fold in the carrots and raisins, if using, just until evenly distributed.

3 **Bake the muffins**
Spoon the batter into the prepared muffin cups, filling them three-quarters full. Bake until the muffins are golden brown and a toothpick inserted into the center of a muffin comes out clean, 15–18 minutes. Let the muffins cool in the pan on a wire rack for 2 minutes. Transfer the muffins to the wire rack, let cool briefly, and serve.

cook's tip

To use this muffin batter for making a carrot cake, butter and flour a 9-inch (23-cm) square baking pan, pour in the batter, and bake as directed for the muffins, but increase the baking time to 45–50 minutes. Let cool completely in the pan on a wire rack, then turn it out and frost with your favorite cream cheese frosting or vanilla buttercream.

cook's tip

It's easy to vary the flavor of these scones. Omit the dried apricots and crystallized ginger and add ¾ cup (3 oz/90 g) dried cherries or cranberries and 1 tablespoon grated lemon or orange zest.

apricot-ginger scones

1 Prepare the baking sheet

Position a rack in the middle of the oven and preheat to 425°F (220°C). Line a rimless baking sheet with parchment (baking) paper.

2 Mix the dough

In a large bowl, stir together the flour, sugar, baking powder, salt, and nutmeg. Using a pastry blender or 2 knives, cut in the butter until the mixture forms coarse crumbs about the size of peas. Stir in the apricots and ginger. In a bowl, whisk together the egg and buttermilk until blended. Add the wet ingredients to the dry ingredients and, using a rubber spatula, stir just until evenly moistened. The dough will be sticky.

3 Shape and bake the scones

Turn out the dough onto a floured work surface and press together gently into a circle about 8 inches (20 cm) in diameter. Using a sharp knife, cut the circle into 6 equal wedges. Place the wedges on the prepared sheet, spacing them about 1 inch (2.5 cm) apart. Bake until the scones are golden brown, 15–17 minutes. Transfer to a wire rack, let cool slightly, and serve warm.

Flour, 1 3/4 cups (9 oz/280 g)

Sugar, 1/3 cup (3 oz/90 g)

Baking powder, 1 tablespoon

Salt, 1/2 teaspoon

Ground nutmeg, 1/4 teaspoon

Unsalted butter, 6 tablespoons (3 oz/90 g) cold, cut into cubes

Dried apricots, 2/3 cup (4 oz/125 g), chopped

Crystallized ginger, 1/4 cup (1 1/2 oz/45 g), chopped

Egg, 1

Buttermilk, 1/2 cup (4 fl oz/ 125 ml)

MAKES 6 SCONES

cherry
turnovers

Frozen puff pastry, 1 sheet, thawed

Pitted sour or sweet cherries, 1 jar (28 oz/875 g)

Brandy or Cognac, 1 teaspoon (optional)

Granulated sugar, ¼ cup (2 oz/60 g)

Flour, 1 tablespoon

Egg, 1

Milk, 1 tablespoon

Coarse sugar such as turbinado, for sprinkling

MAKES 6 TURNOVERS

1 Roll out the puff pastry
Position a rack in the middle of the oven and preheat to 425°F (220°C). Line a rimless baking sheet with parchment (baking) paper. Place the puff pastry sheet on a lightly floured work surface and roll out into a 15-by-10-inch (38-by-25-cm) rectangle. Cut the rectangle in half lengthwise and then cut each half crosswise into 3 squares. Place the squares on the prepared baking sheet.

2 Prepare the cherry filling
Drain the juice from the cherries, place in a bowl, and sprinkle with the brandy, if using. Toss the cherries with the granulated sugar and the flour.

3 Fill and bake the turnovers
In a small bowl, whisk together the egg and milk. Brush a ½-inch (12-mm) border of the egg mixture around 2 adjacent sides of each square. Spoon about 3 tablespoons of the cherry filling almost in the middle of the square. Fold the pastry over the filling to make a triangle and press the edges with a fork to seal. Repeat with the remaining squares. Brush the tops with the remaining egg mixture and sprinkle with the coarse sugar. Bake until the turnovers are puffed and golden brown, 15–18 minutes. Let cool slightly on the baking sheet on a wire rack, and serve warm.

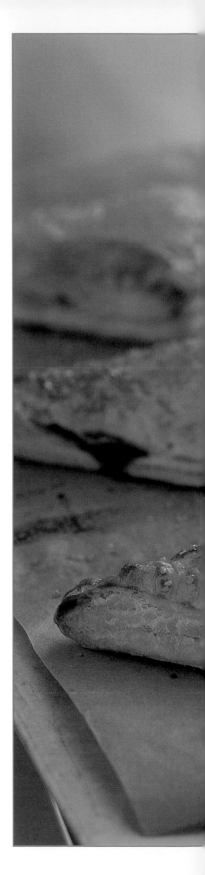

cook's tip

The turnovers may also be filled with other seasonal fruits. In summer, use 2 peaches, peeled, pitted, and cut into slices ½ inch (12 mm) thick. In winter, peel and core 2 pears such as Anjou or Bosc and cut into slices ½ inch (12 mm) thick.

strawberry
shortcakes

1 Prepare the strawberries

In a bowl, combine the strawberries with 2 tablespoons of the sugar and set aside. Position a rack in the middle of the oven and preheat to 425°F (220°C). Line a baking sheet with parchment (baking) paper.

2 Make the shortcakes

In a bowl, stir together the flour, 3 tablespoons of the sugar, the baking powder, and the salt. Using a pastry blender or 2 knives, cut in the butter until the mixture forms coarse crumbs about the size of peas. Add ⅓ cup (3 fl oz/80 ml) of the cream and mix just until evenly moistened. The dough should be soft; if necessary, add an additional 1–2 tablespoons cream. With floured hands, divide the dough into 4 equal portions and shape each into a disk about ¾ inch (2 cm) thick. Place on the prepared sheet, spacing them at least 3 inches (7.5 cm) apart. Bake until golden brown, 12–15 minutes. Transfer the shortcakes to a wire rack and let cool slightly.

3 Fill the shortcakes

Meanwhile, in a bowl, using an electric mixer on high speed, whip the remaining ½–⅔ cup (4–5 fl oz/125–160 ml) cream with the remaining 2 tablespoons sugar and the vanilla until soft peaks form. Split the shortcakes horizontally and place the bottom halves on individual plates. Top with the berries and whipped cream and then with the tops, and serve.

Strawberries, 3 cups (12 oz/ 375 g) hulled and sliced

Sugar, 7 tablespoons (3½ oz/105 g)

Flour, 1 cup (5 oz/155 g)

Baking powder, 1½ teaspoons

Salt, ¼ teaspoon

Unsalted butter, 4 tablespoons (2 oz/60 g) cold, cut into cubes

Heavy (double) cream, 1 cup (8 fl oz/240 ml)

Vanilla extract (essence), ½ teaspoon

SERVES 4

15 minutes
hands-on time

blueberry cobbler

Blueberries, 3 cups
(12 oz/375 g)

Sugar, 3 tablespoons

Flour, 1 cup (5 oz/155 g),
plus 1 tablespoon

Ground cinnamon,
½ teaspoon

Baking powder,
1½ teaspoons

Salt, ¼ teaspoon

Unsalted butter,
4 tablespoons (2 oz/60 g),
cold, cut into cubes

Heavy (double) cream,
6–8 tablespoons
(3–4 fl oz/90–125 ml)

Vanilla ice cream,
for serving (optional)

SERVES 6

1 **Prepare the berries**
Position a rack in the middle of the oven and preheat
to 400°F (200°C). Butter a 9-inch (23-cm) square baking dish.
In a bowl, combine the blueberries, 2 tablespoons of the sugar,
the 1 tablespoon flour, and the cinnamon. Stir gently to mix.
Spread the berry mixture evenly in the prepared dish.

2 **Mix the dough**
In a bowl, combine the remaining 1 cup flour and
1 tablespoon sugar, the baking powder, and the salt. Using
a pastry blender or 2 knives, cut in the butter until the
mixture forms coarse crumbs about the size of peas. Add the
6 tablespoons cream and, using a rubber spatula, stir lightly
until the ingredients are just moistened. The dough should
be soft; if necessary, add an additional 1–2 tablespoons cream.
Using 2 spoons, form mounds of dough about 2 inches
(5 cm) in diameter and place on the top of the berries.

3 **Bake the cobbler**
Bake until the topping is golden brown and the juices
are bubbling around the edges of the dish, about 20 minutes.
Let cool in the dish on a wire rack. Spoon the warm cobbler
onto plates or into bowls, top each with a scoop of ice cream,
if desired, and serve.

cook's tip

Fresh seasonal berries, such as
raspberries, blueberries, and
blackberries, can be frozen for
up to 4 months for future use.
Freeze in a single layer on a
baking sheet and then transfer
the frozen berries to plastic
containers.

cook's tip

When corn is in season, you can
use the kernels from 2 ears for
this recipe. Remove and discard
the husk and silk from each ear.
Stand it upright on a cutting
board and, using a sharp knife,
cut downward between the
kernels and the cob, being careful
not to cut deeply into the cob.

spicy
corn bread

1 **Prepare the baking pan**
Position a rack in the middle of the oven and preheat to 425°F (220°C). Butter a 9-inch (23-cm) square baking pan.

2 **Mix the batter**
In a large bowl, stir together the cornmeal, flour, sugar, baking powder, baking soda, and salt. In another bowl, whisk together the sour cream, eggs, milk, and butter until blended. Add the wet ingredients to the dry ingredients and stir until smooth. Stir in the corn kernels and chiles. Spread the batter evenly in the prepared pan. Sprinkle evenly with the cheese.

3 **Bake the corn bread**
Bake until the corn bread is golden brown and a toothpick inserted into the center comes out clean, about 20 minutes. Let cool slightly in the pan on a wire rack. Cut into squares and serve warm.

Yellow cornmeal, 1 cup (5 oz/155 g)

Flour, 1 cup (5 oz/155 g)

Light brown sugar, 3 tablespoons firmly packed

Baking powder, 1 teaspoon

Baking soda (bicarbonate of soda), 1 teaspoon

Salt, ½ teaspoon

Sour cream, 1 cup (8 oz/ 250 g)

Eggs, 2

Milk, ¼ cup (2 fl oz/60 ml)

Unsalted butter, 4 tablespoons (2 oz/60 g), melted

Corn kernels, 1½ cups (9 oz/280 g), thawed if frozen

Canned roasted green chiles, ⅓ cup (1½ oz/45 g) chopped

Sharp Cheddar cheese, ½ cup (2 oz/60 g) finely shredded

MAKES ONE 9-INCH (23-CM) SQUARE

apricot
clafoutis

Apricots, 1 lb (500 g),
quartered and pitted, about
2 cups

Brandy or Cognac,
2 teaspoons (optional)

Eggs, 2

Milk, ¾ cup (6 fl oz/180 ml)
plus 2 tablespoons

Granulated sugar,
6 tablespoons (3 oz/90 g)

Lemon zest, 1 teaspoon
finely grated

Vanilla extract (essence),
1 teaspoon

Salt, 1 pinch

Flour, ⅓ cup (1½ oz/45 g)

Powdered (icing) sugar,
2 tablespoons

SERVES 4

1 Prepare the baking dishes
Position a rack in the middle of the oven and preheat
to 350°F (180°C). Butter four 1-cup (8–fl oz/250-ml) ramekins
or ovenproof custard cups and place on a rimmed baking
sheet. Place the apricots in the bottom of the dishes, dividing
them evenly, and sprinkle with the brandy, if using.

2 Mix the batter
In a blender, combine the eggs, milk, granulated sugar,
lemon zest, vanilla, salt, and flour. Process until smooth. Pour
the batter over the apricots, dividing it evenly among the dishes.

3 Bake the clafoutis
Bake until each clafouti is puffed and golden brown,
23–25 minutes. Transfer to a wire rack to cool slightly. Dust the
tops with powdered sugar shaken through a sieve, and serve.

cook's tip

Other fruits, such as cherries, plums, or pears, may be used in place of the apricots. Use 2 cups (12 oz/375 g) fruit. Pit the cherries, halve and pit the plums, or peel, halve, and core the pears and cut into chunks.

cook's tip

If you like, use raspberry, cherry, or blueberry jam, instead of blackberry. Store the cookies for up to 5 days in an airtight container at room temperature. You can also freeze them in a heavy-duty resealable plastic bag with waxed paper between the layers for up to 1 month.

coconut-blackberry
cookies

1 Prepare the baking sheets
Position a rack in the middle of the oven and preheat to 350°F (180°C). Line 2 rimless baking sheets with parchment (baking) paper.

2 Mix the batter
In a bowl, using an electric mixer on medium-high speed, beat the egg until light. Gradually add the sugar, vanilla, and lemon zest, beating after each addition. Continue beating until the batter is light and fluffy, about 5 minutes. Using a rubber spatula, fold in the coconut. Drop heaping spoonfuls of the batter onto the prepared baking sheet, spacing them about 1 ½ inches (4 cm) apart. Put a teaspoonful of jam in the center of each cookie, creating a well with the spoon as you add the jam.

3 Bake the cookies
Bake until the cookies are golden brown on the edges, about 15 minutes. Turn off the oven and let the cookies dry in the oven for 10–15 minutes. Let the cookies cool on the baking sheets on wire racks for 5 minutes, then transfer to wire racks to cool completely.

Egg, 1

Sugar, ½ cup (4 oz/125 g)

Vanilla extract (essence), 1 teaspoon

Lemon zest, 2 teaspoons finely grated

Sweetened shredded coconut, 2½ cups (10 oz/ 150 g)

Blackberry jam, ¼ cup (2½ oz/75 g)

MAKES ABOUT
30 COOKIES

cinnamon-walnut coffee cake

Flour, 2 cups (10 oz/315 g)

Baking powder, 1½ teaspoons

Baking soda (bicarbonate of soda), ½ teaspoon

Salt, ¼ teaspoon

Unsalted butter, ½ cup (4 oz/125 g), at room temperature

Sour cream, ¾ cup (6 oz/ 185 g)

Eggs, 2

Orange zest, 1 tablespoon finely grated

Sugar, 1 cup (8 oz/240 g)

Vanilla extract (essence), 1 teaspoon

Ground cinnamon, 2 teaspoons

Walnuts, 1 cup (4 oz/125 g) toasted and chopped

MAKES ONE 9-INCH (23-CM) SQUARE CAKE

1 Mix the batter

Position a rack in the middle of the oven and preheat to 350°F (180°C). Butter a 9-inch (23-cm) square baking pan. In a bowl, stir together the flour, baking powder, baking soda, and salt. In another large bowl, using an electric mixer on medium speed, beat together the butter, sour cream, eggs, orange zest, ¾ cup (6 oz/180 g) of the sugar, and the vanilla until blended. Add the dry ingredients to the wet ingredients and beat on low speed until smooth.

2 Fill the pan

In a bowl, stir together the remaining ¼ cup (2 oz/ 60 g) sugar, the cinnamon, and the walnuts. Spread half of the batter evenly in the prepared pan and sprinkle evenly with half of the walnut mixture. Top with the remaining batter, spreading it evenly, and sprinkle with the remaining walnut mixture.

3 Bake the cake

Bake until the cake is golden brown and a toothpick inserted into the center comes out clean, 25–30 minutes. Let cool slightly in the pan on a wire rack. Cut into squares and serve warm.

cook's tip

A rasp-type grater is ideal for quickly grating orange zest. Be sure to remove only the colored portion of the rind and not the bitter white pith underneath. To bring out the flavorful oil in citrus zest, use the back of a spoon to mash it with ½ teaspoon sugar.

peach brown betty

1 Prepare the bread crumbs

Position a rack in the middle of the oven and preheat to 375°F (190°C). Butter a 9-inch (23-cm) square baking dish. In a bowl, combine the bread crumbs and melted butter, tossing with a fork until the crumbs are evenly moistened. Stir in the brown sugar and nutmeg.

2 Fill the baking dish

Spread half of the peach slices evenly in the prepared dish. Sprinkle evenly with half of the crumb mixture. Spread the remaining peach slices evenly over the crumbs. Sprinkle with the remaining crumb mixture.

3 Bake the brown betty

Cover the dish with aluminum foil. Bake for 15 minutes, then uncover and bake until the topping is golden brown, about 15 minutes longer. Let cool in the dish on a wire rack for 20 minutes before serving. Spoon the warm brown betty into bowls, top each with a scoop of ice cream or a drizzle of cream, and serve.

Dried bread crumbs, 2 cups (8 oz/250 g)

Unsalted butter, 1/3 cup (3 oz/90 g), melted

Light brown sugar, 6 tablespoons (3 oz/90 g) firmly packed

Ground nutmeg, 1/4 teaspoon

Peaches, 6, about 2 lb (1 kg) total weight, peeled, pitted, and sliced

Vanilla ice cream or heavy (double) cream, for serving

SERVES 6

brown sugar blondies

Flour, 1¼ cups (6½ oz/ 200 g)

Baking powder, 1 teaspoon

Baking soda (bicarbonate of soda), ½ teaspoon

Salt, ¼ teaspoon

Unsalted butter, ¾ cup (6 oz/185 g), at room temperature

Light or dark brown sugar, 1 cup (7 oz/220 g) firmly packed

Eggs, 2

Vanilla extract (essence), 1 teaspoon

Sliced (flaked) almonds, ⅔ cup (2½ oz/75 g)

MAKES 16 BLONDIES

1 **Prepare the baking pan**
Position a rack in the middle of the oven and preheat to 350°F (180°C). Butter an 8-inch (20-cm) square baking pan.

2 **Mix the batter**
In a bowl, stir together the flour, baking powder, baking soda, and salt. In a large bowl, using an electric mixer on medium speed, beat together the butter and sugar until creamy. Add the eggs and vanilla and beat until smooth. Add the dry ingredients to the wet ingredients and mix on low speed just until blended. Spread the batter evenly in the prepared pan. Sprinkle evenly with the almonds.

3 **Bake the blondies**
Bake until golden brown and a toothpick inserted into the center comes out almost clean, about 30 minutes. Let cool completely in the pan on a wire rack. Using a sharp knife, cut into squares and serve.

cook's tip

For rich blondie sundaes, cut the
baked blondies into squares,
top each with a scoop of vanilla,
coffee, or toasted almond ice
cream, and drizzle with bittersweet
chocolate sauce.

cook's tip

Because molasses, both light and dark, is very thick, it sticks to the inside of measuring cups. To solve the problem, coat the cup lightly with a neutral-flavored oil, such as canola, before you pour in the molasses. The oil helps the molasses slide free of the cup.

gingerbread
cake

1 Prepare the baking pan

Position a rack in the middle of the oven and preheat to 350°F (180°C). Butter a 9-inch (23-cm) springform pan or cake pan with 2-inch (5-cm) sides. Sprinkle with flour and tap out the excess.

2 Mix the batter

In a bowl, stir together the flour, baking soda, salt, ginger, cinnamon, and pepper. In another bowl, using an electric mixer on medium speed, beat together the butter, brown sugar, and molasses until blended. Add the sour cream and eggs and beat until smooth. Add the dry ingredients to the wet ingredients and mix on low speed until blended. Spread the batter evenly in the prepared pan.

3 Bake the cake

Bake until a toothpick inserted into the center comes out clean, 30–35 minutes. Let the cake cool in the pan on a wire rack for 5 minutes. If using a springform pan, remove the pan sides and slide the cake onto a serving plate. If using a cake pan, run a thin-bladed knife around the edge of the pan and invert the cake onto a serving plate. Let cool slightly, cut into wedges, and serve.

Flour, 2 cups (10 oz/315 g)

Baking soda (bicarbonate of soda), 1 ½ teaspoons

Salt, ¼ teaspoon

Ground ginger, 1 teaspoon

Ground cinnamon, 1 teaspoon

White pepper, ¼ teaspoon

Unsalted butter, ½ cup (4 oz/125 g), melted

Light brown sugar, ½ cup (3 ½ oz/105 g) firmly packed

Light molasses, ½ cup (5 ½ oz/170 g)

Sour cream, ½ cup (4 oz/ 125 g)

Eggs, 2

MAKES ONE 9-INCH
(23-CM) ROUND CAKE

dark chocolate cake

Unsalted butter, ¾ cup
(6 oz/185 g)

**Bittersweet or semisweet
(plain) chocolate,** 8 oz
(250 g), chopped

Unsweetened chocolate,
1 oz (30 g), chopped

Eggs, 6

Salt, ⅛ teaspoon

Granulated sugar, ½ cup
(4 oz/125 g)

Light brown sugar, ½ cup
(3½ oz/105 g) firmly packed

**Cognac, rum, or brewed
double-strength coffee,**
2 tablespoons

Flour, 6 tablespoons
(2 oz/60 g), sifted

Powdered (icing) sugar,
2 tablespoons

MAKES ONE 9-INCH
(23-CM) ROUND CAKE

1 Prepare the cake pan
Position a rack in the middle of the oven and preheat to 350°F (180°C). Line the bottom of a 9-inch (23-cm) springform pan with parchment (baking) paper.

2 Mix the batter
In a small saucepan over medium-low heat, melt the butter and the bittersweet and unsweetened chocolates, stirring to blend. Remove from the heat. In a large bowl, using an electric mixer on high speed, beat the eggs with the salt until thick and pale in color. Gradually beat in the granulated sugar and brown sugar until the mixture is light and doubled in volume, about 5 minutes. Beat in the Cognac. Using a rubber spatula, stir in the melted chocolate mixture and then the flour. Pour the batter into the prepared pan.

3 Bake the cake
Bake until the top is set and a toothpick inserted into the center comes out clean, 30–35 minutes. Let cool in the pan on a wire rack for about 10 minutes. Remove the pan sides and let the cake cool to room temperature. Dust the top with powdered sugar shaken through a sieve, cut into wedges, and serve.

cook's tip

To turn this simple cake into an impressive dinner-party dessert, add a drizzle of raspberry coulis. To make the coulis, purée 2 cups (8 oz/250 g) raspberries in a blender or food processor and strain through a fine-mesh sieve into a bowl. Add sugar and fresh lemon juice to taste.

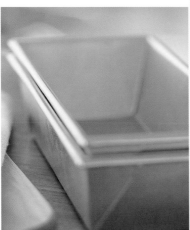

cook's tip

You can bake this same batter in two 8½-by-4½-inch (21.5-by-11.5-cm) loaf pans. Butter and flour the pans as directed, then divide the batter evenly between them. Bake as directed.

banana-honey cake

1 Prepare the baking pan
Position a rack in the middle of the oven and preheat to 350°F (180°C). Butter a 9-inch (23-cm) square baking pan. Sprinkle with flour and tap out the excess.

2 Mix the batter
In a bowl, stir together the flour, baking powder, baking soda, cinnamon, and salt. In another large bowl, using an electric mixer on medium speed, beat together the butter and brown sugar until creamy. Add the honey and beat until blended. Add the eggs, increase the speed to medium-high, and beat until smooth. Add the dry ingredients to the wet ingredients in 2 additions, alternating with the mashed bananas and beating on medium speed after each addition until smooth. Spread the batter evenly in the prepared pan. Sprinkle evenly with the nuts, if using.

3 Bake the cake
Bake until a toothpick inserted into the center comes out clean, 35–40 minutes. Let cool completely in the pan on a wire rack. Cut into squares and serve.

Flour, 2¼ cups (11½ oz/ 360 g)

Baking powder, 1 teaspoon

Baking soda (bicarbonate of soda), 1 teaspoon

Ground cinnamon, 1 teaspoon

Salt, ½ teaspoon

Unsalted butter, ½ cup (4 oz/125 g) plus 2 tablespoons

Light brown sugar, ½ cup (3½ oz/105 g) firmly packed

Honey, ½ cup (6 oz/185 g)

Eggs, 2

Bananas, 2, peeled and mashed

Walnuts or almonds, ⅔ cup (2½ oz/75 g) chopped (optional)

MAKES ONE 9-INCH (23-CM) SQUARE CAKE

lemon
buttermilk bars

Unsalted butter,
6 tablespoons (3 oz/90 g),
at room temperature

Granulated sugar, ¼ cup
(2 oz/60 g), plus ⅔ cup
(5 oz/155 g)

Flour, ⅔ cup (3 oz/90 g),
plus 2 tablespoons

Salt, ⅛ teaspoon

Eggs, 2

Lemon zest, 1 tablespoon
finely grated

Lemon juice, ⅓ cup
(3 fl oz/80 ml)

Buttermilk, ½ cup (4 fl oz/
125 ml)

Powdered (icing) sugar,
for dusting

MAKES 8 BARS

1 **Mix the dough and bake the crust**
Position a rack in the middle of the oven and preheat
to 350°F (180°C). Butter the bottom and sides of an 8-inch
(20-cm) square baking pan. In a large bowl, using an electric
mixer on medium speed, beat together the butter and ¼ cup
granulated sugar until creamy. Add the ⅔ cup flour and the salt
and mix on low speed until blended. Spoon the dough into the
prepared pan and press evenly into the pan bottom. Bake until
the crust is golden, 15–18 minutes.

2 **Make the filling**
Meanwhile, in a large bowl, using the electric mixer
on medium speed, beat the eggs and the remaining ⅔ cup
granulated sugar until blended. Add the remaining 2 tablespoons
flour, the lemon zest and juice, and the buttermilk and beat
until smooth. Pour the filling evenly over the baked crust.

3 **Bake the filling**
Bake until the top of the filling is set and barely browned
at the edges, 20–25 minutes. Let cool completely in the pan
on a wire rack. Cut into 8 bars, dust with powdered sugar shaken
through a sieve, and serve.

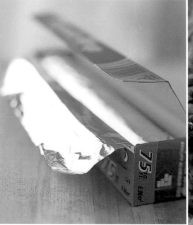

cook's tip

Keep an eye on the crumble
as it bakes. If the topping begins
to brown before the apples are
cooked through, cover the pan
with aluminum foil and reduce
the oven temperature to 350°F
(180°C). This is a great trick
for nearly any baked item that
threatens to darken too much
before it is done.

apple crumble

1 Prepare the apples

Position a rack in the middle of the oven and preheat to 375°F (190°C). Butter a 10-inch (25-cm) pie dish or 9-inch (23-cm) square baking pan or dish. Peel and core the apples, and slice them into a bowl. Add the lemon juice and granulated sugar and toss to coat. Place the apples in the prepared dish and pat them so they are level.

2 Mix the topping

In a bowl, stir together the oats, brown sugar, flour, cinnamon, salt, and walnuts, if using. Drizzle the melted butter over the oat mixture and toss with a fork until evenly moistened. Cover the apples evenly with the topping.

3 Bake the crumble

Bake until the apples are tender when pierced with a knife and the topping is browned, 35–45 minutes. Let cool slightly in the pan on a wire rack. Spoon the crumble into bowls, top each with a dollop of whipped cream or a scoop of ice cream, if desired, and serve.

Large tart apples such as Granny Smith, about 2 lb (1 kg)

Lemon juice, 1 tablespoon

Granulated sugar, 2 tablespoons

Old-fashioned rolled oats, ¾ cup (2½ oz/75 g)

Light brown sugar, ½ cup (3½ oz/105 g) firmly packed

Flour, ⅓ cup (2 oz/60 g)

Ground cinnamon, 1 teaspoon

Salt, 1 pinch

Walnuts, ½ cup (2 oz/60 g) chopped (optional)

Unsalted butter, 6 tablespoons (3 oz/90 g), melted

Whipped cream or vanilla ice cream, for serving (optional)

SERVES 6

lemon-poppyseed shortbread

Unsalted butter, ½ cup
(4 oz/125 g) plus
3 tablespoons

Powdered (icing) sugar,
½ cup (2 oz/60 g)

Lemon zest, 2 teaspoons
finely grated

Flour, 1½ cups (7½ oz/
235 g) plus 2 tablespoons

Poppyseeds, 2 tablespoons

Salt, 1 pinch

MAKES 12 COOKIES

1 **Preheat the oven**
Position a rack in the middle of the oven and preheat
to 325°F (165°C). Have ready a 9-inch (23-cm) cake or pie pan.

2 **Mix the dough**
In a large bowl, using an electric mixer on medium
speed, beat together the butter, sugar, and lemon zest until
creamy. Add the flour, poppyseeds, and salt and beat on low
speed until the dough comes together and is smooth.

3 **Bake the shortbread**
Press the dough evenly into the pan. Lightly prick the
surface all over with a fork. Using a sharp knife, make shallow
cuts halfway through the dough to mark 12 equal wedges.
Bake until firm and barely golden brown around the edges,
45–50 minutes. Let cool completely in the pan on a wire
rack. Carefully invert the shortbread onto a plate, then invert
again onto a cutting board. Cut into wedges, using the marks
to guide you, and serve.

cook's tip

You can prepare the shortbread dough in advance, shape it into a log 2 inches (5 cm) in diameter, wrap it tightly in plastic wrap, and store it in the refrigerator for up to 2 days or in the freezer for up to 2 months. When ready to bake, thaw the dough overnight in the refrigerator, cut the log into slices ¼ inch (6 mm) thick, and bake at 350°F (180°C) until barely golden brown, about 10 minutes.

cook's tip

To separate eggs, place 3 small bowls side by side. Crack the first egg and pull the shell halves apart. Pass the yolk back and forth, letting the white fall into the first bowl. Put the yolk in the second bowl. Transfer the white to the third bowl, and repeat with the remaining eggs. (Always begin with an empty bowl, as a speck of yolk prevents the whites from fully expanding.)

orange chiffon cake

1 Mix the batter

Position a rack in the lower third of the oven and preheat to 325°F (165°C). Have ready an ungreased 10-inch (25-cm) tube pan. Sift together the flour, sugar, baking powder, and salt onto a sheet of parchment (baking) paper or onto a plate. In a large bowl, whisk together the oil, the 6 egg yolks, the orange zest and juice, and ¼ cup (2 fl oz/60 ml) water until well blended. Using a rubber spatula, gently fold the dry ingredients into the wet ingredients until the batter is smooth.

2 Beat the egg whites

In a bowl, using an electric mixer on medium-high speed, beat the 8 egg whites and the cream of tartar until soft peaks form. Using the rubber spatula, gently fold one-half of the whites into the batter until almost blended. Gently fold in the remaining whites just until combined. Pour the batter evenly into the pan.

3 Bake the cake

Bake until a toothpick inserted near the center comes out clean, 50–60 minutes. Invert the pan onto a wire rack and let cool completely, about 1 hour. Run a thin-bladed knife around the edge of the pan and the center tube and invert the cake onto a serving plate. Cut into wedges and serve.

Cake (soft-wheat) flour, 2¼ cups (9 oz/280 g) or all-purpose (plain) flour, 2 cups (8 oz/250 g)

Sugar, 1½ cups (12 oz/ 375 g)

Baking powder, 1 tablespoon

Salt, 1 teaspoon

Canola oil, ½ cup (4 fl oz/ 125 ml)

Eggs, 6 whole, separated, plus 2 whites

Orange zest, 2 tablespoons finely grated

Orange juice, ½ cup (4 fl oz/ 125 ml)

Cream of tartar, ½ teaspoon

MAKES ONE 10-INCH (25-CM) ROUND CAKE

date-pecan bread

Unsalted butter,
3 tablespoons

Dates, 1¼ cups (7½ oz/
235 g) pitted and chopped

**Baking soda (bicarbonate
of soda),** 1 teaspoon

Boiling water, ¾ cup
(6 fl oz/180 ml)

Eggs, 2

Light brown sugar, ¾ cup
(6 oz/185 g) firmly packed

Flour, 1½ cups (7½ oz/
235 g)

Ground cinnamon,
1 teaspoon

Salt, ⅛ teaspoon

Pecans, ¾ cup (3 oz/90 g)
toasted and chopped

MAKES ONE LOAF

1 **Prepare the pan**
Position a rack in the middle of the oven and preheat
to 350°F (180°C). Lightly butter an 8½-by-4½-inch (21.5-by-
11.5-cm) loaf pan.

2 **Mix the batter**
In a bowl, combine the butter, dates, and baking soda.
Add the boiling water and let stand until the dates are softened
and the mixture has cooled slightly, about 5 minutes. Meanwhile,
in another bowl, whisk together the eggs and brown sugar
until blended. Add the date mixture, flour, cinnamon, salt, and
pecans and stir until combined. Spread the batter evenly in
the prepared pan.

3 **Bake the bread**
Bake the bread until a toothpick inserted into the center
comes out clean, about 1 hour. Let cool in the pan on a wire
rack for 10 minutes. Run a thin-bladed knife around the edge
of the pan, invert the loaf onto the rack, and let cool completely.
Cut into slices and serve.

cook's tip

You can use this same batter for making muffins. Line 12 muffin cups with paper liners and spoon in the batter, filling the cups three-quarters full. Bake in a preheated 375°F (190°C) oven until a toothpick inserted into the center of a muffin comes out clean, about 25 minutes.

almond pound cake

1 Prepare the pan

Position a rack in the middle of the oven and preheat to 350°F (180°C). Butter a 10-inch (25-cm) Bundt pan or two 8½-by-4½-inch (21.5-by-11.5-cm) loaf pans. Sprinkle with flour and tap out the excess. In a food processor, process the slivered almonds until finely ground.

2 Prepare the batter

In a large bowl, using an electric mixer on medium speed, beat together the butter and granulated sugar until creamy. Add the eggs one at a time, beating well after each addition. Stir in the vanilla and almond extracts. In another bowl, stir together the flour, baking soda, and salt. Add the dry ingredients to the wet ingredients in 2 additions, alternating with the sour cream and beating on low speed after each addition until smooth. Stir in the ground almonds. Spread the batter evenly in the prepared pan(s). If using loaf pans, sprinkle evenly with the sliced almonds.

3 Bake the cake

Bake until the cake is golden and a toothpick inserted into the center comes out clean, 1–1¼ hours. Let cool in the pan on a wire rack for 10 minutes. Invert the cake onto the rack and lift off the pan. Let the cake cool completely. Dust the top with powdered sugar shaken through a sieve, cut into slices, and serve.

Slivered blanched almonds, 1 cup (4½ oz/ 140 g) toasted

Unsalted butter, 1 cup (8 oz/250 g), at room temperature

Granulated sugar, 2 cups (1 lb/500 g)

Eggs, 6

Vanilla extract (essence), 1½ teaspoons

Almond extract (essence), ½ teaspoon

Flour, 3 cups (15 oz/470 g)

Baking soda (bicarbonate of soda), ¼ teaspoon

Salt, ¼ teaspoon

Sour cream, 1 cup (8 oz/ 250 g)

Sliced (flaked) almonds, ½ cup (2 oz/60 g) (optional)

Powdered (icing) sugar, for dusting

MAKES ONE 10-INCH (25-CM) CAKE OR TWO LOAVES

ricotta tart with cranberries

Dried cranberries, ½ cup (2 oz/60 g)

Triple Sec or other orange-flavored liqueur, 3 tablespoons

Frozen puff pastry, 1 sheet, thawed

Ricotta cheese, 2 cups (1 lb/500 g)

Eggs, 2 large

Granulated sugar, ⅔ cup (5 oz/155 g)

Cornstarch (cornflour), 2 tablespoons

Vanilla extract (essence), 1½ teaspoons

Candied orange peel, ⅓ cup (2 oz/60 g) finely chopped

Powdered (icing) sugar, for dusting (optional)

SERVES 10–12

1 Bake the pastry
Position a rack in the middle of the oven and preheat to 425°F (220°C). Line a baking sheet with parchment (baking) paper. In a small bowl, combine the cranberries and liqueur and let stand until plumped, about 5 minutes. Meanwhile, place the puff pastry sheet on a lightly floured work surface and roll out into a 16-by-12-inch (40-by-30-cm) rectangle. Transfer the rectangle to the prepared pan, fold over the edges 1 inch (2.5 cm) to form a rim, and pinch the edges decoratively. Freeze for 5 minutes, then bake, pricking the dough all over with a fork every 3–4 minutes, until lightly browned, 15–17 minutes.

2 Prepare the filling
Meanwhile, in a food processor, combine the ricotta, eggs, granulated sugar, cornstarch, and vanilla and pulse until blended. Stir in the orange peel and the cranberries and liqueur. When the pastry shell is ready, remove it from the oven and carefully spread the filling evenly in the shell.

3 Bake the tart
Return the tart to the oven and reduce the oven temperature to 350°F (180°C). Bake until the filling is barely puffed and set, about 15 minutes longer. Let cool completely on a wire rack. Refrigerate for at least 1 hour. Dust the tart with powdered sugar shaken through a sieve, if desired. Cut into squares and serve.

cook's tip

Candied orange peel is available in many specialty-food shops. To make your own, remove the peels in strips from 2 oranges. Boil the peels for 5 minutes, drain, and rinse. Boil 1 cup (8 oz/250 g) sugar with ½ cup (4 fl oz/125 ml) water, and 3 tablespoons light corn syrup, stirring. Add the peel and simmer about 1 hour. Drain and let cool slightly on a wire rack, then roll in sugar.

cook's tip

Look for filo dough in 1-lb (500-g) packages in well-stocked markets. Let the package thaw in the refrigerator overnight, then bring to room temperature before removing the sheets. Once the sheets are out of the box, cover them with plastic wrap to prevent them from drying out. Return unused sheets to the refrigerator and use within 3 days.

spinach-feta filo roll

1 Prepare the filling

Position a rack in the middle of the oven and preheat to 375°F (190°C). Line a baking sheet with parchment (baking) paper. In a large frying pan over medium heat, warm the oil. Add the green onions and sauté until softened, about 4 minutes. Add the spinach and sauté until barely wilted, about 1 minute. Remove from the heat and stir in the parsley, nutmeg, and salt and pepper to taste. Let cool slightly. In a large bowl, beat the eggs with a fork until blended and stir in the feta cheese. Add the spinach mixture and stir to combine.

2 Shape the roll

Lay out 1 filo sheet on a work surface and lightly brush with melted butter. Cover with a second sheet and brush it with butter. Repeat with the remaining sheets, brushing each one with butter. Spoon the spinach mixture in a line on a long side of the filo stack, leaving a border of about 1 ½ inches (4 cm) uncovered on the ends and the side. Fold the long border over the filling, fold in the ends, and then gently roll up the dough, encasing the filling.

3 Bake the roll

Place the roll, seam side down, on the prepared pan. Brush the top with butter and sprinkle with the sesame seeds. Bake until the roll is golden brown, 30–35 minutes. Let cool slightly on the pan on a wire rack. Cut into slices and serve.

Olive oil, 1 tablespoon

Green (spring) onions, 8, white and pale green parts, chopped

Baby spinach, 1 lb (500 g), chopped

Fresh flat-leaf (Italian) parsley, 3 tablespoons finely chopped

Ground nutmeg, ½ teaspoon

Salt and freshly ground pepper

Eggs, 3

Feta cheese, 6 oz (185 g) crumbled

Filo dough, 6 sheets, thawed

Unsalted butter, 3–4 tablespoons, melted and slightly cooled

Sesame seeds, 2 tablespoons

SERVES 6

make more to store

chocolate star cookies

CHOCOLATE COOKIE DOUGH

Unsalted butter, 1½ cups (12 oz/375 g), at room temperature

Light brown sugar, 3 cups (21 oz/655 g) firmly packed

Eggs, 3

Vanilla extract (essence), 1 tablespoon

Flour, 3½ cups (17½ oz/ 545 g)

Unsweetened cocoa powder, 1 cup (3 oz/90 g) plus 2 tablespoons

Baking soda (bicarbonate of soda), 1½ teaspoons

Cream of tartar, 1½ teaspoons

Salt, ¾ teaspoon

Coarse sugar, about 4 tablespoons, for sprinkling

MAKES ABOUT 40 COOKIES

makes 3 disks cookie dough total

This easy-to-mix chocolate dough yields three batches of cookies, including these star-shaped cookies and cookie sandwiches that can be filled with frosting or ice cream, on the following pages.

1 Mix the dough
In a large bowl, using an electric mixer on medium speed, beat the butter and brown sugar until creamy. Add the eggs and vanilla and beat until smooth. In another bowl, stir together the flour, cocoa powder, baking soda, cream of tartar, and salt. Add the dry ingredients to the wet ingredients and mix on low speed until blended. Turn out the dough onto a floured work surface. Divide the dough into 3 equal portions, pat each portion into a flat disk, and wrap separately in plastic wrap. Chill 1 disk for at least 1 hour for use now, and store the remaining 2 disks for future use (see Storage Tip, right).

2 Roll out and cut the dough
Position a rack in the middle of the oven and preheat to 350°F (180°C). Line 2 baking sheets with parchment (baking) paper. On a work surface, place the disk between 2 sheets of plastic wrap and roll out about ⅛ inch (3 mm) thick. Using a 2-inch (5-cm) star-shaped (or other) cookie cutter, cut out cookies. Transfer them to the prepared sheets, spacing them 1½ inches (4 cm) apart. Gather the scraps, reroll, and cut out more cookies. Sprinkle the cookies with the coarse sugar.

3 Bake the cookies
Bake until the edges are crisp, 8–10 minutes. Let cool briefly on the sheets, then transfer to a rack to cool completely.

storage tip

The dough disks can be stored
in the refrigerator for up to 3 days
or in the freezer for up to 1 month.
If freezing the disks, wrap in plastic
wrap and then place in heavy-
duty resealable plastic bags. Thaw
overnight in the refrigerator
before using.

cook's tip

For a decorative finish, roll the edges of the sandwiches in semisweet (plain) mini chocolate chips or in finely chopped toasted almonds before freezing.

ice cream
sandwiches

1 Roll out and cut the dough

Position a rack in the middle of the oven and preheat to 350°F (180°C). Line 2 baking sheets with parchment (baking) paper. On a work surface, place the dough disk between 2 sheets of plastic wrap and roll out about ¼ inch (6 mm) thick. Using a 3-inch (7.5-cm) round cookie cutter, cut out cookies. Transfer them to the prepared sheets, spacing them 2 inches (5 cm) apart. Gather the scraps, reroll, and cut out more cookies. You will need 16 cookies.

2 Bake the cookies

Bake until the edges are crisp, 8–10 minutes. Let the cookies cool on the sheets on wire racks for 2 minutes, then transfer to wire racks to cool completely.

3 Make the sandwiches

Place 8 of the cookies, bottom side up, on a work surface. Place a scoop of the ice cream on each cookie. Top with the remaining 8 cookies, bottom side down, and gently press each sandwich together to flatten the ice cream evenly. Place each sandwich in a small resealable plastic bag, seal the bag, and freeze for at least 1 hour. To keep the sandwiches longer, place them in heavy-duty resealable plastic bags and store in the freezer for up to 3 weeks.

Chocolate Cookie Dough (page 70), 1 disk, at cool room temperature

Ice cream, 1 ½ pt (24 fl oz/ 750 ml) flavor of your choice, slightly softened

MAKES 8 SANDWICHES

mocha sandwich cookies

Chocolate Cookie Dough (page 70), 1 disk, at cool room temperature

Unsalted butter, 1 ½ tablespoons, at room temperature

Powdered (icing) sugar, ½ cup (2 oz/60 g)

Unsweetened cocoa powder, 2 teaspoons

Brewed double-strength coffee or espresso, 1 tablespoon

MAKES ABOUT
20 COOKIES

1 **Roll out and cut the dough**
Position a rack in the middle of the oven and preheat to 350°F (180°C). Line 2 baking sheets with parchment (baking) paper. On a work surface, shape the dough disk into a log about 2 inches (5 cm) in diameter. Using a sharp knife, cut into slices ⅛ inch (3 mm) thick. Transfer them to the prepared sheets, spacing them 1 ½ inches (4 cm) apart.

2 **Bake the cookies**
Bake until the edges are crisp, 8–10 minutes. Let the cookies cool on the sheets on wire racks for 2 minutes, then transfer to wire racks to cool completely.

3 **Fill the cookies**
To make the frosting, in a small bowl, cream the butter with a fork. Sprinkle the sugar and cocoa over the butter and stir until blended. Stir in the coffee until smooth. Place half of the cookies, bottom side up, on a work surface. Using an icing spatula, spread the frosting on the cookies, dividing it evenly. Top with the remaining cookies, bottom side down. Let stand at room temperature until set, about 1 hour, and serve.

cook's tip

Instead of filling the cookies
with mocha frosting, you can
spread them with raspberry jam
or mascarpone cheese lightly
sweetened with powdered (icing)
sugar and flavored with a few
drops of framboise or Cognac.

strawberry–cream cheese tart

TART DOUGH

Flour, 3 cups (15 oz/470 g)

Powdered (icing) sugar,
⅓ cup (1½ oz/45 g)

Unsalted butter, 1½ cups
(12 oz/375 g), cold, cut
into cubes

Ice water, ⅓ cup (3 fl oz/
80 ml)

Cream cheese, 6 oz (185 g),
at room temperature

Heavy (double) cream,
¾ cup (6 fl oz/180 ml)

Powdered (icing) sugar,
¼ cup (1 oz/30 g)

Vanilla extract (essence),
1 teaspoon

Strawberries, 2 cups (8 oz/
250 g), stems removed
and berries halved lengthwise

MAKES ONE 9½-INCH
(24-CM) TART

makes 3 disks
tart dough total

With this recipe, you'll have enough dough for two large tart shells, plus a quartet of tartlet shells. The dough comes together quickly in a food processor and bakes up to a sweet, crumbly, buttery finish.

1 Make the dough
In a food processor, combine the flour, the ⅓ cup powdered sugar, and the butter. Pulse until the mixture forms coarse crumbs about the size of peas. Add the water and process just until fine crumbs form. Transfer to a work surface, divide into 3 equal portions, and press each into a disk. Set 1 disk aside and wrap 2 disks in plastic wrap for future use (see Storage Tip, right).

2 Bake the tart shell
Position a rack in the middle of the oven and preheat to 425°F (220°C). Place the disk on a lightly floured surface and roll out into a 10½-inch (26-cm) round. Transfer it to a 9½-inch (24-cm) tart pan with a removable bottom. Fold the overhang back over itself and press it into the sides of the pan to make a sturdy rim. Freeze for 5 minutes. Bake until golden brown, 15–18 minutes. Transfer the pan to a wire rack and let cool.

3 Finish the tart
In a large bowl, using an electric mixer on medium speed, beat the cream cheese until light. Add the cream, the ¼ cup sugar, and the vanilla and beat until smooth, 2–3 minutes. Spread the filling evenly in the tart shell. Place the berries, cut side down, on the filling. Cover and chill for about 2 hours. Remove the pan rim, cut the tart into wedges, and serve.

storage tip

The dough disks can be stored in the refrigerator for up to 3 days or in the freezer for up to 1 month. If freezing, wrap in plastic wrap and then place in resealable plastic bags; thaw overnight in the refrigerator before using. Or, roll out the dough and line a tart pan, place the pan in a plastic bag, and refrigerate or freeze until needed.

cook's tip

If you don't have a double boiler, you can easily create one by resting a stainless-steel bowl on top of a saucepan partially filled with simmering water. Make sure the bottom of the bowl does not touch the water.

lemon
tart

1 Bake the tart shell

Position a rack in the middle of the oven and preheat to 425°F (220°C). Place the dough disk on a lightly floured surface and roll out into a 10½-inch (26-cm) round. Gently transfer the dough to a 9½-inch (24-cm) tart pan with a removable bottom. Fold the overhang back over itself and press it into the sides of the pan to make a sturdy rim. Freeze for 5 minutes. Bake until golden brown, 15–18 minutes. Let cool on a wire rack.

2 Prepare the filling

In a small bowl, dissolve the cornstarch in 2 tablespoons water. In the top pan of a double boiler, whisk together the eggs, lemon zest and juice, sugar, and cornstarch mixture. Place over simmering water in the bottom pan and whisk until thickened, about 10 minutes. Remove from the heat and whisk in the butter.

3 Finish the tart

Pour the warm filling into the baked tart shell. Refrigerate for at least 2 hours or for up to 24 hours. Remove the pan rim and cut the tart into wedges. Top each serving with a dollop of whipped cream, if desired, and serve.

Tart Dough (page 76), 1 disk, at cool room temperature

Cornstarch (cornflour), 1 tablespoon

Eggs, 5

Lemon zest, 2 teaspoons finely grated

Lemon juice, ⅔ cup (5 fl oz/ 160 ml)

Sugar, ¾ cup (6 oz/185 g)

Unsalted butter, 6 tablespoons (3 oz/90 g), cut into small pieces

Whipped cream, for serving (optional)

MAKES ONE 9½-INCH (24-CM) TART

chocolate-raspberry tartlets

Tart Dough (page 76),
1 disk, at cool room
temperature

Unsalted butter,
4 tablespoons (2 oz/60 g)

Bittersweet chocolate,
6 oz (185 g), finely chopped

**Brewed double-strength
coffee or espresso,**
1 teaspoon

Eggs, 3

Granulated sugar, ⅔ cup
(5 oz/155 g)

Vanilla extract (essence),
1 teaspoon

Raspberries, 1⅓ cups
(5½ oz/170 g)

Powdered (icing) sugar,
for dusting

MAKES 4 TARTLETS

1 **Partially bake the tartlet shells**
Position a rack in the middle of the oven and preheat
to 425°F (220°C). Divide the dough disk into 4 equal portions.
Pat each piece evenly into the bottom and up the sides of
a 4½-inch (11.5-cm) tartlet pan with a removable bottom.
Freeze for 5 minutes. Place the pans on a baking sheet and
bake until very lightly browned, about 5 minutes. Let cool on
the baking sheet on a wire rack. Reduce the oven temperature
to 375°F (190°C).

2 **Prepare the filling**
In a saucepan over low heat, combine the butter,
chocolate, and coffee and heat, stirring, until melted and
thoroughly blended, about 3 minutes. In a bowl, whisk the eggs
until blended. Gradually whisk in the granulated sugar. Stir
in the chocolate mixture and vanilla. Pour the filling into the
partially baked tart shells, dividing it evenly.

3 **Bake the tartlets**
Bake until the filling is set, about 15 minutes. Transfer
the tartlets to a wire rack and let cool. Arrange the raspberries
on top of the filling. Dust the tartlets with powdered sugar
shaken through a sieve. Remove the pan rims, slide the tarts
from the pan bottoms onto 4 plates, and serve.

cook's tip

To make a large tart, roll out the dough and line a 9½-inch (24-cm) tart pan. Freeze for 5 minutes, then prebake the crust in a 425°F (220°C) oven for 10 minutes. Let cool completely, then pour the filling into the shell and bake at 375°F (190°C) until set, about 25 minutes. Top with the berries and dust with the powdered sugar as directed.

cook's tip

To prepare neat pear slices for a tart, halve the pear lengthwise and cut away the stem. Using a melon baller, scoop out and discard the core. Finally, peel the pear halves and cut lengthwise into thin slices.

pear-custard tart

1 Partially bake the tart shell

Position a rack in the middle of the oven and preheat to 425°F (220°C). Place the dough disk on a lightly floured surface and roll out into a 10½-inch (26-cm) round. Gently transfer the dough to a 9½-inch (24-cm) tart pan with a removable bottom. Fold the overhang back over itself and press it into the sides of the pan to make a sturdy rim. Freeze for 5 minutes. Bake until very lightly browned, 8–10 minutes. Let cool in the pan on a wire rack.

2 Make the filling

Arrange the pear slices in the partially baked tart shell. In a bowl, using an electric mixer on medium speed, beat the eggs until thick and pale in color. Beat in the sugar. Add the butter, cream, lemon zest, flour, and vanilla and mix well. Pour the mixture evenly over the pears.

3 Bake the tart

Bake the tart for 15 minutes. Reduce the oven temperature to 400°F (200°C) and bake until the filling is set and the crust is golden brown, about 25 minutes longer. Let cool slightly in the pan on a wire rack. Remove the pan rim. Cut the tart into wedges and serve.

Tart Dough (page 76), 1 disk, at cool room temperature

Pears such as Bartlett, Anjou, or Bosc, 4, peeled, halved, cored, and thinly sliced

Eggs, 2

Sugar, ⅔ cup (5 oz/155 g)

Unsalted butter, 2 tablespoons, melted

Heavy (double) cream, 2 tablespoons

Lemon zest, 1 teaspoon finely grated

Flour, 3 tablespoons

Vanilla extract (essence), 1 teaspoon

MAKES ONE 9½-INCH (24-CM) TART

pecan
tart

Tart Dough (page 76),
1 disk, at cool room
temperature

Eggs, 3

Light brown sugar, ½ cup
(3½ oz/105 g) firmly packed

Dark corn syrup, 1 cup
(10 fl oz/315 ml)

Vanilla extract (essence),
1 teaspoon

Unsalted butter,
4 tablespoons (2 oz/60 g),
melted

Pecan halves, 1½ cups
(6 oz/185 g)

Whipped cream, for serving
(optional)

MAKES ONE 9½-INCH
(24-CM) TART

1 **Partially bake tart shell**
Position a rack in the middle of the oven and preheat
to 425°F (220°C). Place the dough disk on a lightly floured
surface and roll out into a 10½-inch (26-cm) round. Gently
transfer the dough to a 9½-inch (24-cm) tart pan with a
removable bottom. Fold the overhang back over itself and
press it into the sides of the pan to make a sturdy rim. Freeze
for 5 minutes. Bake until very lightly browned, 8–10 minutes.
Let cool in the pan on a wire rack.

2 **Prepare the filling**
In a large bowl, whisk together the eggs, brown sugar,
corn syrup, and vanilla until blended. Whisk in the melted
butter. Stir in the pecans. Pour the filling into the partially
baked tart shell.

3 **Bake the tart**
Bake until the filling is set but is still slightly soft in the
center, 40–45 minutes. Let cool slightly in the pan on a wire
rack. Remove the pan rim. Cut the tart into wedges, top each
with a dollop of whipped cream, if desired, and serve.

cook's tip

For a Chocolate-Pecan Tart variation, add 1 cup (6 oz/185 g) semisweet (plain) or bittersweet chocolate chips to the filling mixture along with the pecans. Bake as directed.

berry
galette

FLAKY PASTRY DOUGH

Flour, 4 cups (1¼ lb/625 g)

Salt, 1 teaspoon

Unsalted butter,
1½ cups (12 oz/375 g) plus
3 tablespoons, cut into cubes

Ice water, ¾ cup (6 fl oz/
180 ml)

**Blackberries, blueberries,
or a mixture,** 4 cups
(1 lb/500 g)

Lemon juice, 2 tablespoons

Sugar, ¼ cup (2 oz/60 g)

Flour, 3 tablespoons

MAKES ONE 9-INCH
(23-CM) GALETTE

makes 3 disks
pastry dough total

A food processor makes this flaky pastry dough in a snap. The recipe yields enough dough for three pies or galettes, such as this berry-filled galette and the quiche and pies that follow.

1 Mix the dough

In a food processor, combine the flour and salt and pulse briefly to mix. Scatter the butter over the top and pulse just until the mixture forms coarse crumbs about the size of peas. Drizzle the ice water over the flour mixture and pulse just until the dough starts to come together. Transfer to a work surface, divide into 3 equal portions, and press each into a flat disk. Set 1 disk aside and wrap 2 disks in plastic wrap for future use (see Storage Tip, right).

2 Roll out the dough

Position a rack in the middle of the oven and preheat to 425°F (220°C). Line a baking sheet with parchment (baking) paper. Place the dough on a lightly floured surface and roll out into a 13-inch (33-cm) round. Fold the round in half, transfer to the prepared sheet, then unfold the round.

3 Fill and bake the galette

In a bowl, lightly toss together the berries, lemon juice, sugar, and flour. Spoon the filling onto the dough, leaving a 2-inch (5-cm) border uncovered around the edge. Fold the edge up and over the filling, forming loose pleats. Bake until the filling is bubbling and the pastry is golden brown, about 25 minutes. Transfer the galette to a wire rack and let cool slightly. Cut into wedges and serve.

storage tip

The dough disks can be stored in
the refrigerator for up to 3 days
or in the freezer for up to 1 month.
If freezing the disks, wrap in plastic
wrap and then place in heavy-
duty resealable plastic bags;
thaw overnight in the refrigerator
before using.

cook's tip

You can substitute various vegetables for the bacon in the quiche filling, such as cooked small broccoli florets or chopped broccoli, sautéed sliced leeks, or chopped cooked spinach. Use about 1½ cups (6 oz/185 g).

classic quiche

1 Partially bake the pastry shell

Position a rack in the middle of the oven and preheat to 425°F (220°C). Place the dough disk on a lightly floured surface and roll out into a 12-inch (30-cm) round. Fold the dough round in half and transfer to a 9-inch (23-cm) pie dish. Unfold the round and ease it into the dish, patting it firmly into the bottom and up the sides. Trim the edges to form a 1-inch (2.5-cm) overhang. Fold the overhang under itself and pinch to create a high edge on the rim of the pan. Using a fork, prick the bottom of the dough a few times. Freeze for 5 minutes. Bake until lightly golden, about 10 minutes. Let cool on a wire rack. Reduce the oven temperature to 375°F (190°C).

2 Prepare the filling

In a saucepan over medium heat, fry the bacon until crisp, about 5 minutes. Transfer to paper towels to drain. Sprinkle half of the cheese evenly over the partially baked pastry shell. In a large bowl, whisk the eggs until blended. Whisk in the half-and-half, nutmeg, and salt. Stir in the bacon and the remaining cheese. Pour into the partially baked pastry shell.

3 Bake the quiche

Bake until the filling is set and slightly puffed and the crust is golden brown, 30–35 minutes. Let cool briefly on a wire rack. Cut into wedges and serve warm.

Flaky Pastry Dough (page 86), 1 disk, at cool room temperature

Bacon, 8 strips, chopped

Gruyère or Swiss cheese, 1½ cups (6 oz/185 g) shredded

Eggs, 4

Half-and-half (half cream) or milk, 1¾ cups (14 fl oz/ 430 ml)

Ground nutmeg, ¼ teaspoon

Salt, ½ teaspoon

MAKES ONE 9-INCH (23-CM) QUICHE

pumpkin
pie

**Flaky Pastry Dough
(page 86),** 1 disk, at cool
room temperature

Eggs, 3

Light brown sugar, ¾ cup
(6 oz/185 g) firmly packed

Ground cinnamon,
½ teaspoon

Ground ginger, ½ teaspoon

Ground allspice,
¼ teaspoon

Salt, ½ teaspoon

Pumpkin purée, 1 can
(15 oz/470 g)

**Half-and-half (half cream)
or milk,** 1½ cups (12 fl oz/
375 ml)

Whipped cream, for serving
(optional)

MAKES ONE 9-INCH
(23-CM) PIE

1 **Partially bake the pastry shell**
Position a rack in the middle of the oven and preheat
to 425°F (220°C). Place the dough disk on a lightly floured
surface and roll out into a 12-inch (30-cm) round. Fold the
dough round in half and transfer to a 9-inch (23-cm) pie pan.
Unfold the round and ease it into the pan, patting it firmly into
the bottom and up the sides. Trim the edges to form a 1-inch
(2.5-cm) overhang. Fold the overhang under itself and pinch
to create a high edge on the rim of the pan. Using a fork, prick
the bottom of the dough a few times. Freeze for 5 minutes.
Bake until lightly golden, about 10 minutes. Let cool completely
on a wire rack. Reduce the oven temperature to 375°F (190°C).

2 **Prepare the filling**
In a large bowl, whisk the eggs until blended. Add the
sugar, cinnamon, ginger, allspice, and salt and mix well. Mix
in the pumpkin purée and half-and-half until well blended. Pour
into the partially baked pastry shell.

3 **Bake the pie**
Bake until the filling is set and the crust is golden brown,
35–40 minutes. Let cool briefly on a wire rack. Cut into
wedges, top each serving with a dollop of whipped cream,
if desired, and serve.

cook's tip

You can line the pie pan with the dough and partially bake the pie shell in advance. Cover and store at room temperature for up to 1 day, or freeze in a heavy-duty resealable plastic bag for up to 3 weeks and thaw before filling.

cook's tip

You can omit the streusel topping
and use a second dough disk to
make a double-crust pie. Roll out
the second disk as you did the
first one. Lay the second pastry
round on top of the filling and
trim even with the bottom. Roll
both overhangs under and flute
the edge. Make 3 or 4 steam
vents in the center of the top
crust, and bake as directed.

rhubarb
pie

1 **Roll out the dough**
Position a rack in the middle of the oven and preheat to 400°F (200°C). Place the dough disk on a lightly floured surface and roll out into a 12-inch (30-cm) round. Fold the dough round in half and transfer to a 9-inch (23-cm) pie dish or pan. Unfold the round and ease it into the dish, patting it firmly into the bottom and up the sides. Trim the edges to form a 1-inch (2.5-cm) overhang. Fold the overhang under itself and crimp to make a decorative edge.

2 **Prepare the filling and the streusel**
In a small bowl, dissolve the cornstarch in 1 tablespoon water. In a large bowl, lightly toss the rhubarb with the granulated sugar. Stir in the cornstarch mixture. Spoon the filling into the dough-lined dish. To make the streusel, in another bowl, stir together the flour and the brown sugar. Using a pastry blender or 2 knives, cut in the butter until the mixture is crumbly. Sprinkle the streusel over the filling.

3 **Bake the pie**
Bake until the juices are bubbling and the crust is golden brown, 40–45 minutes. Let cool briefly on a wire rack. Cut into wedges, top each with a scoop of ice cream or a dollop of whipped cream, if desired, and serve.

Flaky Pastry Dough (page 86), 1 disk, at cool room temperature

Cornstarch (cornflour), 3 tablespoons

Rhubarb, 1 lb (500 g), trimmed and chopped (about 5 cups/12 oz/375 g)

Granulated sugar, 1 1/2 cups (12 oz/375 g)

Flour, 2/3 cup (4 oz/120 g)

Light brown sugar, 2/3 cup (5 oz/155 g) firmly packed

Unsalted butter, 1/2 cup (4 oz/120 g), cold, cut into pieces

Vanilla ice cream or whipped cream, for serving (optional)

MAKES ONE 9-INCH (23-CM) PIE

the smarter cook

Lots of people enjoy baking, but many don't think they have the time. That problem is quickly solved with a collection of easy baking recipes and some savvy advance planning. In the following pages, you'll find everyday time-saving tools and techniques. You'll learn how to prep ingredients like a professional baker, how to shop for everything from flour to eggs, and how to store all your baked goods so they stay fresh and delicious.

You'll also find tips on how to keep a well-stocked pantry, so you are ready to bake whenever you have time. We'll show you how to mix up a big batch of pastry dough to use some the same night and freeze the rest for later use. Plus, you'll find dozens of tips on how to manage your time and organize your kitchen—the keys to becoming a smarter cook.

get started

One of the best things about baking is that once your pantry and refrigerator are stocked with all the baker's staples (pages 104–107), you can prepare nearly any recipe with only a quick shopping trip to pick up one or two fresh or specialty items. You'll also need to give some thought to how baking fits into your busy schedule, and to what you should bake, considering both the season and the occasion.

plan your baking

- **Look at the whole week.** During the weekend, take time to think about the week ahead. Is there a special event coming up—a birthday that needs a cake, or a school bake sale that needs a few dozen cookies? Will this be a hectic workweek when some quickly reheated muffins might come in handy for a speedy breakfast? Think about what you'll be serving during the week, too. A rich, elaborate evening meal might end perfectly with a piece of fruit, while a casual soup-and-salad supper can leave you with extra time to get a batch of cookies in the oven.

- **Plan your time.** Once you've picked what you'd like to bake, decide when you'll have time to make it. Think about what can be made the night before or what can be frozen in advance.

- **Get everyone involved.** Enlist the help of kids and other family members in deciding what to bake, and then get everyone involved in putting together the recipe. Make helping out in the kitchen, from greasing pans to mixing batter to washing bowls, a special treat.

- **Bake on the weekend.** Baked goods hot from the oven always taste best, but busy weekday mornings seldom include enough time to make a batch of muffins or scones. If possible, prepare your baked goods over the weekend and freeze leftovers to enjoy during the week. Make a double batch of banana cake or cherry turnovers, and then freeze individual servings for future use. Do the time-consuming part of a recipe, like making and rolling out pie dough, when you have extra time, and chill or freeze the dough for quick baking later in the week (see page 107 for freezing tips).

OCCASIONS

brunch
Cheddar-Chive Biscuits (page 18)
Raspberry-Lemon Muffins (page 21)
Cinnamon-Walnut Coffee Cake (page 40)
Almond Pound Cake (page 63)
Classic Quiche (page 89)

fun for kids
Chocolate Brownie Cookies (page 17)
Cherry Turnovers (page 26)
Strawberry Shortcakes (page 29)
Chocolate Star Cookies (page 70)
Ice Cream Sandwiches (page 73)

tea time
Butter Pecan Cookies (page 10)
Apricot-Ginger Scones (page 25)
Brown Sugar Blondies (page 44)
Gingerbread Cake (page 47)

fit for dessert
Blueberry Cobbler (page 32)
Apricot Clafoutis (page 36)
Lemon Tart (page 79)
Pear-Custard Tart (page 83)

celebrate
Dark Chocolate Cake (page 48)
Orange Chiffon Cake (page 59)
Chocolate-Raspberry Tartlets (page 80)
Berry Galette (page 86)

Using fresh seasonal ingredients is an easy way to ensure great flavor and to match what you bake with the mood and weather of the moment. While what's in season will vary depending on your location, here's a general guide to year-round baking.

spring Celebrate the return of warm weather and the beginning of the growing season by showcasing the early fruits of spring, such as rhubarb and strawberries, in tarts and pies.

summer The long, hot days of summer deliver sweet berries and juicy stone fruits. Shortcakes, pies, crisps, and cobblers are particularly well suited to the season's abundance. Fill them with apricots, cherries, peaches, nectarines, plums, blackberries, blueberries, or raspberries, or a mixture of berries.

autumn As the days grow shorter and the nights turn crisp, fill the cookie jar. Warm up with spicy treats scented with cinnamon, ginger, and nutmeg and packed with apples, cranberries, nuts, pears, and pumpkin.

winter Holiday festivities mean dinner parties, cookie exchanges, and long, lazy brunches. Indulge in chocolate cakes and cookies. Dried fruits fill in while most fruit trees are bare, and tropical fruits and citrus add brightness to long winter days. Fill the house with baked treats flavored with chocolate, dried fruits, tropical fruits such as mangoes and pineapples, and citrus fruits such as lemons, limes, tangerines, and oranges.

dress up dessert

From a scoop of ice cream to a fresh fruit sauce, rounding out the plate with an easy addition can turn a simple baked treat into a special dessert. High-quality ice creams and sauces are quick and delicious ways to dress up cakes and tarts, while freshly whipped cream is always a popular garnish. Fresh fruits can be prepared a few hours ahead of time and refrigerated, while dried fruits can be poached several days in advance.

- **Ice cream** A small scoop of high-quality vanilla ice cream goes well with nearly every dessert, whether it's a slice of warm pecan pie or a square of gingerbread or pound cake. Choose basic flavors—vanilla, coffee, chocolate, caramel—for the most versatility.

- **Whipped cream** Real whipped cream takes only a few minutes to make, and its silky richness is unmatched by commercial products. In a chilled bowl, combine 1 cup (8 fl oz/250 ml) very cold cream, 2 tablespoons sugar, and ½ teaspoon vanilla extract (essence). Using an electric mixer on medium-high speed, beat until medium peaks form, about 3 minutes. Cover and refrigerate until ready to serve or for up to 2 hours.

- **Fresh fruit** Serve a plate of cookies with sliced peaches or nectarines, cubed mangoes, or mixed berries. Add a drizzle of lemon juice or a favorite liqueur such as amaretto or Grand Marnier. Or, top cake slices with fresh berries or a few slices of fruit.

- **Sauces & syrups** A little good-quality chocolate, butterscotch, or caramel sauce can make any cake look professional. Look for a brand made from natural ingredients. Warm the sauce on the stove top or in a microwave. Drizzle it on a slice of cake and nestle a small scoop of ice cream or a dollop of whipped cream alongside.

- **Cookie sandwiches** Match your cookies with a complementary ice-cream flavor, such as chocolate cookies with mint chip or ginger-molasses cookies with vanilla. Let the ice cream soften, spread a layer ½ inch (12 mm) thick on the bottom of half the cookies, top with the remaining cookies, bottom side down, and place in a resealable plastic bag. Freeze for at least 1 hour.

tools & techniques

You don't need a lot of fancy gadgets to be a good baker, but you do want to have some basic tools specifically used for baking, such as baking sheets and pans. And while you can always improvise, you'll save time and energy by having the right equipment. Buy good-quality equipment for the best results, and organize your kitchen so that the tools you use frequently are close at hand.

tools used for baking

- **Bowls** A set of nesting bowls is used for holding ingredients and mixing batters and doughs. Choose tempered glass, stainless steel, or ceramic.

- **Mixer** A handheld mixer with detachable beaters works well for creaming butter, whipping egg whites and cream, and mixing batters. A stand mixer, usually with three attachments—paddle, whip, and dough hook—can accommodate larger amounts of batter and leave your hands free for adding ingredients.

- **Food processor** A food processor makes quick work of chopping nuts and grating cheese, and is a great choice for making pastry dough.

- **Rasp grater** A file-style grater with a handle is the most efficient tool for zesting citrus. It is also ideal for finely grating hard cheeses.

- **Rolling pin** Usually made of wood, these heavy cylinders are used for rolling out pastry and cookie doughs. American-style pins with handles are the easiest to use.

- **Spoons, rubber spatulas & whisks** Wooden spoons are ideal for mixing batters, rubber spatulas are used for scraping bowls clean and folding in delicate ingredients. A heat-resistant rubber spatula is also a good addition to your set of baking tools. Whisks—particularly balloon whisks—are handy for creating smooth mixtures and for whipping cream and egg whites.

- **Cooling rack** A footed wire rack holds hot baked goods above the work surface to encourage rapid cooling without condensation.

MEASURING

measuring cups & spoons Use clear glass or plastic cups with measurements on the side for measuring liquid ingredients, and use a set of metal or plastic cups in graduated sizes for measuring dry ingredients. The same set of spoon measures are used for measuring small amounts of liquid and dry ingredients.

liquid Place a liquid measuring cup on a level surface and pour in the liquid to the appropriate line. Always check the measurement at eye level. For spoon measures, fill to the rim.

dry Dip the correct-sized dry measuring cup or spoon into the ingredient, filling it to overflowing, and then sweep off the excess with the straight edge of a table knife. Never shake or pack the measuring cup or spoon.

To measure brown sugar, which is the only exception to this rule, fill the correct-sized cup with the sugar and pack it down firmly with the back of a spoon. Continue adding sugar and packing it down until the sugar is level with the rim. When the cup is turned over, the sugar should fall out in the shape of the cup.

baking pans These come in many shapes and sizes and are usually made of tempered glass or heavy-gauge aluminum. For the recipes in this book, you'll need a square baking pan, a loaf pan, a Bundt or tube pan (which has a hollow, cylindrical stem in the middle), a muffin pan, and a two-part springform pan, which has sides secured by a latch that is popped open after baking for easy unmolding of cakes.

baking sheets Sometimes called cookie sheets, these large rectangular metal pans have a shallow rim, or they have one or two ends with very low, flared rims for sliding cookies onto cooling racks. It's handy to have two sheets, so you can fill one sheet while the other one is in the oven. Heavier baking sheets are generally better, as they bake and brown cookies and other items more evenly than thinner sheets.

pie pans & dishes These round pans and dishes are made of metal, tempered glass, or ceramic and have gently sloping sides that make them perfect for pies and quiches. Glass pie dishes have the advantage of allowing you to see if the bottom crust is browned.

ramekins These single-serving, ovenproof porcelain dishes, which look like mini soufflé dishes, are useful for making individual cakes and desserts.

tart pans Available in many sizes and shapes, shallow metal tart pans usually have fluted edges and come with a removable bottom for easy unmolding.

easy techniques

The recipes in this book can be easily mastered even by novice bakers. If you haven't done a lot of baking, familiarize yourself with some common terms and techniques that you'll need to know before you start.

- **Beating** Mixing ingredients together vigorously until they are smooth and thoroughly amalgamated is called beating. It's also the term used for whipping air into heavy (double) cream or egg whites. Egg whites and cream can be beaten with a whisk, a handheld electric mixer, or the whip attachment on a stand mixer.

- **Cutting in** Recipes for biscuits, scones, and pastry dough often call for cutting chilled butter into the flour mixture. To cut in the butter, chop it into cubes. If making the dough by hand, cut the butter into the flour using a pastry blender or two table knives. The mixture should be coarse with pea-sized pieces of butter. If using a food processor, pulse the cold butter into the flour in short bursts, until the same consistency is reached.

- **Creaming** Beating softened butter with sugar or other ingredients is called creaming. It mixes air into the butter, which helps the mixture rise when baked. It also blends the sugar into the butter, forming a smooth mixture. Beat the butter with a wooden spoon, a handheld mixer, or the paddle attachment of a stand mixer for several minutes until creamy. Gradually add the sugar and beat for a few minutes until fluffy.

- **Folding** Delicate ingredients, such as beaten egg whites, should always be folded, rather than stirred, into heavier mixtures. This keeps the air bubbles intact that help the cake or other item rise in the oven. With a rubber spatula, scoop the lighter ingredient on top of the heavier one. Then, using a circular motion, gently draw the spatula down through the center of the bowl and up the side. Continue, rotating the bowl as you fold, until the mixture is nearly uniform.

- **Stirring** When making most cakes and muffins, you must stir in the flour as gently as possible to ensure a tender crumb. Use a wooden spoon or a handheld or stand mixer (with the paddle attachment) on the lowest speed just until no patches of flour are visible.

baked goods storage

Most baked goods can be stored at room temperature in airtight containers or in plastic wrap for a couple of days. Some items require refrigeration, however, or can be frozen for longer storage.

Freezing quick breads & cookies

To store cookies, cakes, muffins, and other quick breads for more than a couple of days, freeze them. Let them cool completely after baking, then wrap tightly in aluminum foil, plastic wrap, or freezer paper. Store small items like cookies and muffins in resealable plastic freezer bags, expelling as much air as possible from the bag before sealing. Thaw at room temperature or in the refrigerator. To serve them, warm in the oven at 250°F (120°C) until heated through.

Storing tart & pastry dough

Store unbaked tart and pie dough, tightly wrapped or in a resealable plastic bag, in the refrigerator for 2 to 3 days. To freeze pastry dough, unbaked pie or tart shells, and filled unbaked fruit pies, wrap in aluminum foil, plastic wrap, or freezer paper and freeze for up to 4 months. Remember to mark the package with the date before stowing it away. Frozen pie and tart shells can go directly from the freezer to the oven without thawing. Frozen unbaked fruit pies can also be baked without thawing. Bake the pie in a preheated 425°F (220°C) oven for the first 30 minutes, then reduce the temperature to 350°F (180°C) for the remainder of the baking. The pie will probably take about 15 minutes longer to bake than a similar fruit pie that was not frozen.

Refrigerating pies, tarts & cakes

In general, pies and tarts with custard-based fillings, such as pumpkin pie, do not freeze well. Once they are made, store them in the refrigerator, unless they will be eaten within a few hours of baking. Remove them from the refrigerator about 30 minutes before serving to bring them to room temperature. Refrigerate cakes with whipped cream frostings immediately and those with butter frostings within 2 hours. Serve the former chilled and the latter at room temperature.

TESTING DONENESS

cakes & quick breads are done when a wooden toothpick inserted into the center comes out clean. The center should spring back when pressed lightly with a fingertip, and the edges of the cake or bread should have pulled away from the sides of the pan.

pie & tart pastry should be golden brown. Fruit fillings should be bubbly and juicy, while custard fillings should be set.

cookies should generally be firm and lightly browned around the edges. Always check the recipe for specific tips on testing doneness.

COOLING BAKED GOODS

Always cool baked goods on a footed wire rack, which allows air to circulate on all sides. The items will cool faster and they are less likely to become soggy.

For most cakes and quick breads, let cool in the pan for 5–10 minutes, then, if necessary, loosen the edges with a table knife. Place the wire rack upside down on top of the cake or bread. Using pot holders, invert the pan and the rack and shake gently to unmold the cake or bread onto the rack. Cool pies and tarts in their pans on a rack.

To cool most cookies, transfer them from the baking sheet to the rack with a spatula, or slide them from the rimless end of a cookie sheet onto the rack.

shop smarter

Using the freshest produce and the highest-quality ingredients available gives you a head start toward great flavor and healthier eating. You should be able to get nearly all the items you need for the recipes in this book at a well-stocked supermarket. For some items, such as high-quality chocolate or crystallized ginger, try shopping at specialty-food stores, which can offer more and better choices.

MAKE A SHOPPING LIST

Nothing is more frustrating than deciding you have time to bake and finding out that you are out of an essential ingredient, such as baking powder. Or, perhaps you have found yourself standing in the supermarket not being able to remember whether you used up all the brown sugar the last time you made cookies.

To save yourself from these shopping headaches, create a list template on your computer for both your pantry and your refrigerator (see lists of staples, pages 106 and 107) and fill it in during the week before you go shopping. Use the following categories to keep your lists organized.

pantry Check the pantry and list items that need to be restocked to make the recipes you plan to bake during the week.

fresh These are ingredients you'll use within the week. It's helpful to divide the list into supermarket sections, such as produce and dairy.

miscellaneous This covers specialty items for a specific recipe, such as shredded coconut or crystallized ginger, or items you use only occasionally, such as liqueurs.

Flour The recipes in this book were tested using all-purpose (plain) flour, the most common flour found in markets. It is available bleached (chemically treated) and unbleached. Unbleached flour, which contains more protein and has a more pleasing flavor, is recommended.

Sugars Granulated sugar is the most common sugar used in baking. Brown sugar, which is colored with molasses, comes in two styles: light and the more strongly flavored dark. Choose well-sealed packages and squeeze gently to be sure the sugar is loose and moist.

Dairy Check the expiration date on dairy products before purchasing them. For the best flavor, use whole milk when baking.

Eggs Eggs come in a variety of sizes and grades, according to their age and the condition of their shell. Most baking recipes use grade A large eggs. Look for the expiration date on the carton, and always open the lid to check for cracked or damaged eggs.

Nuts Buy nuts in small quantities to ensure freshness.

Produce Always ask which fruits and vegetables are at their peak of flavor and ripeness. If there is a regular farmers' market in your area, get in the habit of visiting it once a week. It's an excellent way to stay in touch with what is in season, and you'll often find good deals on bumper-crop produce. Choose fruits and vegetables that are free of bruises and blemishes and feel heavy for their size. Imported, out-of-season fruit has often been picked long before ripeness to survive long shipping periods; usually, it will be more expensive and less flavorful. Avoid most imported fruits, as they are often picked before they are ripe to survive long shipping, and are typically less flavorful than seasonal fruit.

the well-stocked kitchen

Smart cooking is all about being prepared. Keeping your pantry, refrigerator, and freezer well stocked and organized means you won't have to run to the store at the last minute when you are ready to bake. Get into the habit of keeping track of what's in your kitchen, and you'll find you can shop less frequently and spend less time in the store when you do.

On the pages that follow, you'll find a guide to the essential ingredients to have on hand for baking, both for general use and based upon the recipes found in this book. You will also find tips on how to keep these ingredients fresh and store them efficiently. Use this guide to stock your kitchen now and you'll be able to make any recipe in this book by picking up just a few fresh ingredients in a quick shopping trip.

the pantry

The pantry is typically a closet or one or more cupboards in which you store flour, sugar, dried spices, extracts (essences) and other flavorings, dried fruits, nuts, and canned and bottled or jarred goods. Make sure that it is relatively cool, dry, and dark when not in use. It should also be a good distance from the stove, as heat can dry out pantry staples, especially spices, robbing them of their flavor and aroma.

pantry storage

- **Spices & flavorings** The flavor of dried spices start to fade after about 6 months. Buy spices in small quantities so you can use them up and replace them often. Ethnic markets and natural-foods stores often sell spices in bulk. They are usually fresher and much less expensive than the prepackaged spices on supermarket shelves. For extracts (essences) and flavorings, buy the highest quality you can afford, and avoid artificial or imitation flavorings. Store them in airtight containers in a cool, dry place—never near the stove.

- **Nuts & dried fruits** Store most nuts and all dried fruits in airtight containers for up to 1 month. To keep them longer, refrigerate them for up to 6 months, or freeze them for up to 9 months.

- **Chocolate & cocoa** Buy the best-quality chocolate and cocoa powder that you can afford. Unsweetened chocolate, which is also known as baking chocolate, contains no sugar and is hard and extremely bitter. Bittersweet and semisweet (plain) chocolate have some sugar and cocoa butter added, making them smoother and sweeter. They are not interchangeable with unsweetened chocolate. To store chocolate, wrap it in aluminum foil and plastic wrap; it will keep for up to 1 year. Temperature fluctuations can cause chocolate to develop a chalky white film, sometimes referred to as the "bloom." Although the chocolate will look less appealing, its quality is unaffected, and the color disappears as soon as the chocolate is melted. Always use unsweetened cocoa powder, not hot-cocoa mix, for baking; it will keep, tightly sealed, for up to 1 year.

STOCK YOUR PANTRY

take inventory Remove everything from the pantry and sort the items by type. Take inventory of what you have using the Pantry Staples list (page 106).

clean Wipe the shelves clean and reline them with shelf paper, if needed.

check freshness Look for expiration dates on all the items and discard anything that has passed its date. Also, throw away any items that have a stale or otherwise questionable appearance, odor, or flavor.

list & shop Make a list of all the items that you need to replace or buy, and then make a trip to the store to buy everything on your list.

restock Put all your pantry items away, organizing them as much as possible by type of ingredient so everything is easy to find. Place newer items behind older ones, so you'll use the older ones first. Keep staples that you use often toward the front of the pantry as well.

mark the date Write the date on the package of each new item before putting it away, so you'll know when you bought it and when to replace it.

review your recipes Look over the recipes you plan to make during the week to see what ingredients you'll need.

check your staples Take a look in your pantry to be sure you have the ingredients you'll need on hand.

make a list Draw up a list of any items that are missing, so you can replace them the next time you go shopping.

rotate items Mark the date on your new purchases, then place them in the pantry. As you put them away, check what you already have and rotate the items as needed, moving the oldest ones to the front so they will be used first.

OVENS

The recipes in this book were tested using a conventional oven. Any oven can have hot spots; also, large pans and baking sheets can block heat and create variances in temperature between racks.

To ensure what you are baking cooks evenly, check occasionally and rotate the pans as needed. If you are baking two baking sheets of cookies at the same time, switch them between the oven racks and rotate them 180 degrees midway through baking.

An accurate oven temperature is very important to successful baking. Use an oven thermometer to check whether or not your oven is heating correctly.

Flours & grains Whole-grain flours, such as whole wheat (wholemeal), and stone-ground cornmeal can develop a stale or rancid odor and flavor if stored at room temperature for more than a few weeks. To keep them longer, store in airtight containers in the freezer. Even all-purpose (plain) flour can become stale over time, so buy no more than you will use in 6 months and store in airtight containers. If any grain product or flour smells off or stale, or develops small, gummy "threads" on the top, discard it.

Leavening agents Baking powder, baking soda (bicarbonate of soda), and cream of tartar are chemical leaveners that interact with liquid or acidic ingredients in a batter to produce bubbles of carbon dioxide. As a cake or other dessert bakes, the bubbles expand, causing the cake to rise. Mark the date of purchase on the containers and store baking powder and baking soda for no more than 6 months and cream of tartar for no more than 1 year. (If you store a box of baking soda in the refrigerator to combat odors, keep a separate box in the pantry for baking.) To test if a leavener is still effective, scoop out a spoonful and add a little water to it. It should fizz vigorously.

Sweeteners Store all types of sugar in airtight containers. Brown sugar, which has been mixed with molasses to add flavor and give it a soft, packable consistency, hardens when exposed to air. If this happens, warm it gently in a low oven or a microwave until it softens. Powdered (icing) sugar is made from granulated sugar that has been milled until very fine and mixed with a small amount of cornstarch (cornflour) to prevent clumping. If lumps do form, pass it through a sieve. If honey crystallizes, stand the jar in a saucepan of warm water over low heat or warm in the microwave until it liquefies.

Spirits Buy good-quality spirits in small bottles. You never need more than a spoonful or two and cheaper versions can taste harsh or contain artificial ingredients that impart an off flavor. A sprinkle of orange-scented Grand Marnier or almond-flavored amaretto can turn a simple fruit salad into an elegant dessert, especially when paired with homemade shortbread or pound cake. Keep spirits stored tightly closed. They will keep indefinitely, but have the best flavor if used within 6 months.

PANTRY STAPLES

SPICES & FLAVORINGS

allspice, ground

almond extract (essence)

cinnamon, ground

ginger, ground

nutmeg, ground

pepper, white

poppy seeds

salt

sesame seeds

vanilla extract (essence)

NUTS & DRIED FRUITS

almonds

apricots

cranberries

currants

dates

pecans

raisins

walnuts

FLOURS & GRAINS

cake (soft-wheat) flour

cornmeal

cornstarch (cornflour)

flour, unbleached all-purpose

(plain)

oats, rolled

LEAVENING AGENTS

baking powder

baking soda (bicarbonate of soda)

cream of tartar

SWEETENERS

corn syrup

honey

molasses, light

sugar, dark brown

sugar, granulated

sugar, light brown

sugar, powdered (icing)

sugar, raw or coarse

CHOCOLATE & COCOA

chocolate chips

chocolate, semisweet (plain)

chocolate, unsweetened

cocoa powder, unsweetened

SPIRITS

brandy

cognac

rum

Triple Sec or orange liqueur

CANNED & JARRED FOODS

cherries, sweet or tart

pumpkin purée

roasted green chiles

MISCELLANEOUS

blackberry jam

bread crumbs, dried

canola oil

coconut, sweetened shredded

ginger, crystallized

olive oil

orange peel, candied

WEIGHTS & EQUIVALENTS

ALL-PURPOSE (PLAIN) FLOUR, UNSIFTED

¼ cup	=	1½ oz/45 g
⅓ cup	=	2 oz/60 g
½ cup	=	2½ oz/75 g
1 cup	=	5 oz/155 g

ALL-PURPOSE (PLAIN) FLOUR, SIFTED

¼ cup	=	1 oz/30 g
⅓ cup	=	1½ oz/45 g
½ cup	=	2 oz/60 g
1 cup	=	4 oz/125 g

GRANULATED SUGAR

2 tablespoons	=	1 oz/30 g
3 tablespoons	=	1½ oz/45 g
¼ cup	=	2 oz/60 g
⅓ cup	=	3 oz/90 g
½ cup	=	4 oz/125 g
1 cup	=	8 oz/250 g

BROWN SUGAR, FIRMLY PACKED

¼ cup	=	2 oz/60 g
⅓ cup	=	2½ oz/75 g
½ cup	=	3½ oz/105 g
1 cup	=	7 oz/220 g

BUTTER

1 tablespoon	=	½ oz/15 g
2 tablespoons	=	1 oz/30 g
3 tablespoons	=	1½ oz/45 g
4 tablespoons	=	2 oz/60 g
⅓ cup	=	3 oz/90 g
½ cup	=	4 oz/125 g
1 cup	=	8 oz/250 g
2 cups	=	1 lb/500 g

PRODUCE

apples

apricots

blackberries

blueberries

carrots

peaches

pears

raspberries

rhubarb

strawberries

DAIRY

butter, unsalted

buttermilk

Cheddar cheese

cream cheese

cream, heavy (double)

eggs

Feta cheese

fresh ricotta

Gruyère

half-and-half (half cream)

milk, whole

sour cream

FROZEN FOODS

filo dough

frozen blueberries

frozen blackberries

frozen corn kernels

ice cream

puff pastry

cold storage

Once you have organized your pantry, you can apply the same principles to your refrigerator and freezer. Both are good for storing many staples (left), plus they are used for chilling some baked goods and unbaked pastry dough and pies (page 100).

general tips

- Remove items a few at a time and give the refrigerator and freezer a thorough cleaning with warm, soapy water.

- Discard old or questionable items.

- Use the Cold Storage Staples list (left) as a starting point to decide what you need to buy or replace.

- Keep the temperature of the freezer below 0°F (-18°C), and avoid packing it too tightly. You want air to circulate freely so that foods freeze quickly, which helps preserve their flavor and texture. Let food cool to room temperature, pack in airtight containers, and then label with the name and date. Thaw baked goods in a microwave or at room temperature.

fruit storage

Depending on the season, keep a variety of fruits on hand, either in the refrigerator or on the countertop. You can keep pears, plums, mangoes, peaches, nectarines, pineapples, and kiwifruits at room temperature to ripen and soften and then refrigerate them. Always store bananas at room temperature. Other fruits, including apples and berries, should be stored in the refrigerator's crisper drawer.

Berries are particularly fragile, and should be used within a day or two of purchase. To prevent them from developing mold or being crushed, line a shallow plastic container with a paper towel, cover evenly with a single layer of unrinsed berries, cover tightly, and refrigerate; rinse just before using.

index

Oxmoor House

OXMOOR HOUSE

Oxmoor House books are distributed by Sunset Books
80 Willow Road, Menlo Park, CA 94025
Telephone: 650 321 3600 Fax: 650 324 1532

Vice President/General Manager Rich Smeby
National Accounts Manager/Special Sales Brad Moses
Oxmoor House and Sunset Books are divisions of
Southern Progress Corporation

WILLIAMS-SONOMA
Founder & Vice-Chairman Chuck Williams

THE WILLIAMS-SONOMA FOOD MADE FAST SERIES
Conceived and produced by Weldon Owen Inc.
814 Montgomery Street, San Francisco, CA 94133
Telephone: 415 291 0100 Fax: 415 291 8841

In collaboration with Williams-Sonoma, Inc.
3250 Van Ness Avenue, San Francisco, CA 94109

Photographers Tucker + Hossler
Food Stylist Jennifer Straus
Food Stylist's Assistants Luis Bustamante, Max La Rivière-Hedrick
Prop Stylist Leigh Nöe
Text writer Stephanie Rosenbaum

Library of Congress Cataloging-in-Publication data is available.
ISBN 0-8487-3138-7

WELDON OWEN INC.

Chief Executive Officer John Owen
President and Chief Operating Officer Terry Newell
Chief Financial Officer Christine E. Munson
Vice President International Sales Stuart Laurence
Creative Director Gaye Allen
Publisher Hannah Rahill
Art Director Kyrie Forbes Panton
Senior Editor Kim Goodfriend
Editor Emily Miller
Designer and Photo Director Andrea Stephany
Designer Kelly Booth
Assistant Editor Juli Vendzules
Production Director Chris Hemesath
Color Manager Teri Bell
Production and Reprint Coordinator Todd Rechner

A WELDON OWEN PRODUCTION
Copyright © 2006 by Weldon Owen Inc. and Williams-Sonoma, Inc.
All rights reserved, including the right of reproduction in
whole or in part in any form.

Set in Formata
First printed in 2006
10 9 8 7 6 5 4 3 2 1
Color separations by Bright Arts Singapore
Printed by Tien Wah Press

Printed in Singapore

ACKNOWLEDGMENTS
Weldon Owen wishes to thank the following people for their generous support in producing this book:
Davina Baum, Heather Belt, Carrie Bradley, Kevin Crafts, Ken DellaPenta, Judith Dunham,
Alexa Hyman, Marianne Mitten, Sharon Silva, Nick Wagner, and Kate Washington.

Photographs by Bill Bettencourt: pages 8–9, 20–21 (recipe), 26–27 (recipe), 30–31, 38–39 (recipe), 42–43,
44–45 (recipe), 64–65, 66–67, 68–69, 78 (upper left), 81 (upper right), 82–83 (upper left and recipe),
84–85 (upper right and recipe), 86–87, 88–89 (upper left and recipe), 90–91, 92–93

Cover photograph styled by Kevin Crafts: Almond Pound Cake, page 63

A NOTE ON WEIGHTS AND MEASURES
All recipes include customary U.S. and metric measurements. Metric conversions are based on
a standard developed for these books and have been rounded off. Actual weights may vary.